INTERNATIONAL LIBRARIANSHIP

INTERNATIONAL LIBRARIANSHIP

Developing Professional, Intercultural, and Educational Leadership

Edited by

CONSTANTIA CONSTANTINOU

MICHAEL J. MILLER

KENNETH SCHLESINGER

STATE UNIVERSITY OF NEW YORK PRESS

Cover photo: The three traditional structures that comprise the LLP library at Ngwerere School (credit: Jane Kinney Meyers).

Published by
State University of New York Press, Albany

© 2017 State University of New York

All rights reserved

Printed in the United States of America

No part of this book may be used or reproduced in any manner whatsoever without written permission. No part of this book may be stored in a retrieval system or transmitted in any form or by any means including electronic, electrostatic, magnetic tape, mechanical, photocopying, recording, or otherwise without the prior permission in writing of the publisher.

For information, contact
State University of New York Press, Albany, NY
www.sunypress.edu

Production, Laurie D. Searl
Marketing, Anne M. Valentine

Library of Congress Cataloging-in-Publication Data

Names: Constantinou, Constantia, 1964– editor. | Miller, Michael J., 1966– editor. | Schlesinger, Kenneth, editor.
Title: International librarianship : developing professional, intercultural, and educational leadership / edited by Constantia Constantinou, Michael J. Miller, and Kenneth Schlesinger.
Description: Albany : State University of New York Press, [2017] | Includes bibliographical references and index.
Identifiers: LCCN 2016021652 (print) | LCCN 2016053976 (ebook) | ISBN 9781438463674 (hardcover : alk. paper) | ISBN 9781438463667 (pbk. : alk. paper) | ISBN 9781438463681 (e-book)
Subjects: LCSH: International librarianship—Case studies.
Classification: LCC Z672.3 I585 2017 (print) | LCC Z672.3 (ebook) | DDC 020.6/21—dc23
LC record available at https://lccn.loc.gov/2016021652

10 9 8 7 6 5 4 3 2 1

CONTENTS

ILLUSTRATIONS

FIGURES

TABLE

FOREWORD

Librarianship is a field of learning, of assisting others in their efforts to expand their boundaries and extend themselves. These twelve essays take us on journeys that our colleagues have embarked on to Central America, the Caribbean, Central Europe, Africa, the Mediterranean, and Asia, all in the name of learning and supporting librarian communities in other areas of the world. They traveled for periods ranging from weeks to months as Fulbright Scholars, Fulbright Senior Specialists, Peace Corps volunteers, and as members of a Fulbright-Hays Seminar, with support from grants and professional organizations or collaborations established through local connections and philanthropic organizations.

Their travels were educational, fulfilling, and productive. They designed and launched new services related to reference and library instruction, delivered lectures, taught collection development and research classes, designed training for Peace Corps volunteers, organized conferences, wrote grants and development documents, drafted strategic plans, designed curricula, delivered story times, cataloged collections, edited conference proceedings, and wrote articles for international library publications.

Their experiences led to friendships, new connections, and return trips to continue and expand their work. They bring their wisdom back to us, so that we may learn about the challenges of walking along political, social, cultural, historical, and religious boundaries while respecting the values and expressions of others. And they relate how they prepared for their work. They not only have the requisite technical and practical skills to bring to the new settings, they learn to pack and they study languages, history, literature, and cuisine. They bring patience, trust, diplomacy, and flexibility, and they acquire confidence. They expand their feelings of empathy and their ability to communicate with a wide range of patrons, including local leaders. They have to be independent, and sometimes they are lonely.

They find support, challenges, and sometimes, the unexpected. One librarian worked to establish a new archive at the Steve Biko Centre, only to encounter opposition from South African archivists. Another's host family discouraged him from communicating with female family members. Yet another found a meaningful message in a sign along a rural road in Cyprus: Library = Democracy + Critical Thinking.

While they appreciate their new friends and colleagues, they return with a renewed respect for the American library. They reflect on the strengths, routines, and innovations of libraries they know in the United States, from advocacy efforts to interlibrary loan, online catalogs, self-service copy machines, circulation systems and policies, Friends of the Library and volunteer organizations, and the comparatively greater salaries of American counterparts. They leave us with advice:

- Be respectful but do not be shy.
- Try to establish a cooperative connection and avoid being perceived as patronizing.
- Leaders of international library development initiatives need to question what they bring to developing countries as outsiders.
- Collective negotiation of timelines and schedules necessitates a calm approach, sensitivity, and flexibility.

Please join me in appreciating these stories, but do not stop there. I invite you to start your own international connections. A fine place to begin is to reach out to a professional library organization, such as the International Relations Round Table of the American Library Association.

Dr. Loriene Roy
School of Information
University of Texas at Austin

EDITORS' INTRODUCTION

With the world growing smaller, we inevitably wish to turn outward and engage more fully with others, extending the spirit of service that is a core element of librarianship. International librarianship has been framed as a trend that follows the early-twentieth-century rise of global non-governmental organizations pursuing advocacy in an era of transcultural, social, and political change (Witt, 2014). As such, librarians presently concern themselves with complex issues and corresponding responses that address global requisites for cost-effective information access, literacy support, patron empowerment, and international development.

This collection of essays originated from our impulse to share the successes and challenges of international librarianship. As Fulbright recipients, the editors have benefitted from participating as leaders and learners in our respective assignments around the world. As a group, we wanted to celebrate the legacy of service inherent in a Fulbright fellowship award by offering insights into substantial and provocative projects. Ultimately, we desire to inform other librarians about extraordinary opportunities for leadership, professional growth, and service learning in a global setting.

As a consequence, we aspired to solicit narratives of the disciplinary and cultural competencies and the emotional intelligence required to engage in international librarianship. We hoped to be informed of the impact—both personal and professional—of the use of best practices outside daily and local settings. Echoing concerns about global leadership within the profession (Asselin, 2011), we wanted to learn about the impact of international librarianship on information access and overall education in emerging and developing countries. Lastly, we wanted to understand how these unique and exceptional experiences are being creatively applied on return to the local service environment. How has our learning been repurposed and extended, informing new practices and influencing collaboration within and across the profession, the home institution, and our communities?

We're both gratified and inspired by the response and engagement of our colleagues. Please join us for an exciting international journey into avenues of information need across library type and institution, brimming with unexpected challenges, unanticipated setbacks, discoveries, insights, and triumphs, all of which resulted in professional enrichment. These experiences highlight a range of collaborations that support educational partnerships, program initiatives, and professional development, and ultimately assist international citizens with their own agency and empowerment.

Yours in international librarianship,
Constantia Constantinou
Michael J. Miller
Kenneth Schlesinger

REFERENCES

Asselin, M. (2011). Internationalism as leadership in IASL research: Accomplishments and directions. *School Libraries Worldwide, 17*(2), 13–24.

Witt, S. (2014). *Agents of change: The rise of international librarianship and the age of globalization*. Retrieved from doi:10.1353/lib.2014.0006.

ACADEMIC EXCHANGES

THE TORONTO–ADDIS ABABA ACADEMIC COLLABORATION LIBRARY SCIENCE PROGRAM

A Case Study in Global Librarianship in Ethiopia

Sandra Kendall

The Toronto–Addis Ababa Academic Collaboration Library Science Program (TAAAC-LSP) is modelled on the Toronto–Addis Ababa Psychiatry Project (TAAPP) (http://www.psychiatry.utoronto.ca/toronto-addis-ababa-psychiatry-project-taapp/), which was formally established in 2003 to support the first psychiatry residency program in Ethiopia. This project is a collaborative program between the University of Toronto (UofT) and Addis Ababa University (AAU) designed to help train psychiatry residents in Ethiopia.

With a population of over 80 million supported by 2,000 doctors, Ethiopia's increase in the number of psychiatrists from seven to forty over a period of ten years demonstrates the success of this psychiatry project. More than twenty educational teams have traveled to Addis Ababa two to three times per year for one-month periods. Each team consists of two UofT psychiatric faculty and one UofT psychiatry resident. TAAPP has developed a template for an educational partnership that has been embraced by AAU as a model for Western educational partnerships. This successful template of partnership between the UofT Department of Psychiatry and AAU has been adopted by other medical specialists travelling to Ethiopia (Alem, Pain, Araya, & Hodges, 2010).

The Ethiopian academic community's request for expansion into a broader university-to-university educational partnership resulted in the subsequent collaboration between AAU and UofT in June 2008. Called the Toronto–Addis Ababa Academic Collaboration (TAAAC) (http://www.taaac.com), there are now nineteen different programs, divisions, and departments involved in initiating educational partnerships for allied health master's and PhD programs.

The primary focus of TAAAC is the development of tertiary professional training programs. It is the umbrella organization housing and facilitating all educational partnerships between their newly developed counterparts at AAU. TAAAC serves to assist AAU in building and strengthening capacity and sustainability in medical specialties and other health and nonhealth professional training programs. Currently there are partnerships at various stages of development, including anesthesia, dentistry, emergency medicine, engineering, family medicine, history, internal medicine, library science, medical imaging, nursing, obstetrics and gynecology, pediatrics, pharmacy, psychiatry, rehabilitation sciences, and surgery.

TAAAC-LSP is an essential component of this educational collaborative. Partners in this collaborative include AAU's chief librarian; the chief medical librarian at Tikur Anbessa (the Black Lion Hospital), a fully-affiliated teaching hospital; Sandra Kendall, director of library services at Mount Sinai Hospital, who initiated the program; and Sandra Langlands, former director of UofT's Gerstein Science and Information Centre.

The vision created by TAAAC-LSP partners, developed during on-site meetings in Ethiopia, incorporates the recognition that further enhancement of medical library services and clinical librarianship at AAU is essential for the broad medical education collaboration now under way. Importantly, TAAAC-LSP deliverables are determined, directed, and driven by our Ethiopian colleagues.

Although we believe this is the only certain way to establish a successful partnership—consisting of negotiated goals based on the real needs and capacities of all stakeholders—we still believe it is unusual to meet, refine, and tailor these goals in person. We expect that establishing relationships at the beginning of the project, supported by frequent emails for distance learning and on-site visits, will enable the introduction of new ideas and library methods. Armed with specific country knowledge, this library program innovatively aims to maximize and expand the field of library science, taking into account AAU's current challenges of Internet access and bandwidth; the current knowledge, training, and learning interests of the Ethiopian librarians; and the requirements of faculty and trainees. An important innovation of TAAAC-LSP is providing annual on-site professional training sessions over a five-year period. Based on a model established by TAAPP, this is likely to foster positive training relationships capable of flexibly responding to shifts in learning needs.

Further, to ensure sensitivity to the educational relationships and requisites between all the trainers and learners, there is ongoing evaluation of the partnership. Feedback and responsiveness are necessary to introduce new ideas and capabilities and extend the capacity of library services. We believe that the TAAAC-LSP model can be broadened to include all trainers and trainees at AAU, including medical and nursing students. It could also be applied to other AAU faculties, Ethiopian medical schools and universities, and ultimately to other English-speaking African schools and universities.

Guidelines established by the TAAAC Governance Committee and followed by each discipline require prospective candidates to attend predeparture cultural briefing sessions. These mandatory sessions, designed by TAAAC governance leads Clare Pain (MD, MSc, FRCPC, associate professor at UofT Department of Psychiatry) and Atalay Alem

FIGURE I.1. New Central Medical Library, 2015 (Credit: Carla Hagstrom)

(MD, PhD, professor, Department of Psychiatry, AAU consultant psychiatrist, Amanuel Hospital Addis Ababa), assist in evaluating attendees for their cultural readiness as program participants.

> Cultural competence training and cultural awareness is of paramount importance for those working in any international or clinical setting. . . . Furthermore, those in any clinical setting must understand language barriers, how to work with translators, cultural differences, cultural understanding, and trust, among other cultural concerns. (Unite for Sight, 2014)

Inclusion in TAAAC-LSP requires more than the skill set of clinical librarianship or knowledge of HINARI, the electronic library established by the World Health Organization to provide biomedical and health literature to developing countries (Van Essen, C., Cartledge, P., Kyamanywa, P., & Manirakiza, A., 2012). Although medical library skills are considered a basic necessity, soft skills are quite exacting and have on occasion been difficult to ensure. Being a well-travelled library professional does not necessarily qualify one as an appropriate cultural fit. Experience working with others, flexibility, and demonstrated team-building skills help ensure continued success.

Nonattendance at TAAAC briefings has resulted in embarrassment for the team. Insensitivity and inappropriate verbal and nonverbal communication can put the TAAAC-LSP relationship on a tenuous footing. As a consequence, the required professional competencies combined with cultural sensitivities must go hand in hand.

During predeparture cultural briefings, various team members and trainers who have successfully fostered educational relationships share their insights. They openly discuss topics such as racial awareness, health and safety, appropriate attire, religion, languages, expectations, housing, food and beverages, precautionary and required travel inoculations, medical considerations, cellphones and SIM cards, and access to the Internet. The consistent emphasis is on never being rude, never expressing impatience, and never losing your temper.

TAAAC-LSP is driven by our AAU professional colleagues and gently guided by the expertise of University of Toronto Libraries (UTL), when requested. During the initial 2008 assessment of Black Lion Hospital's medical library, a number of issues were identified. Our partnership agreement listed deliverables, such as improving access to current print and electronic resources, as well as discoverability of hard-to-locate full-text clinical journals. Ethiopian librarians and health practitioners requested introduction to best-evidenced resources, evidence-based practices, and the role of the clinical librarian.

On returning from my first trip to Ethiopia in 2008, armed with a partnership agreement between Mount Sinai Hospital library and Black Lion Hospital library, I requested an update of my job description to ensure that efforts expended on this partnership were formally recognized in my organization and viewed as part of my responsibilities. Mount Sinai Hospital proudly supports health as a global initiative. Their support and encouragement has been extremely beneficial to this project. As part of a fully affiliated teaching and research hospital, I also wanted to guarantee ongoing support and commitment from UTL. In January 2013, the original partnership agreement was extended to a UTL- and AAU-library-endorsed Letter of Agreement.

To date, we continue to work on accomplishing all the deliverables specified in the original 2008 partnership agreement. The expectation for TAAAC-LSP to provide current medical textbooks resulted in shipping of over 3,000 relevant medical texts to Black Lion. The project required its own critical path, which had to be set up to manage shipment of textbooks. Subject disciplines and titles had to be identified and located. Each donated text required an identifying sticker to ensure its successful movement through customs on both ends. Each shipped title is entered into UTL's SIRSI catalog, allowing for an accurate inventory.

We have succeeded in approaching vendors to donate both print resources and access to online databases. In 2010, TAAAC-LSP and UofT Books with Wings (BWW) raised over $CN6,000 towards funding shipments of donated books. A private donor selected a core medical library print collection, which was shipped to Ethiopia in 2011. Through this donor, we were introduced to our new shipping partner, the Canadian Blind Mission, which certified that donations arrive safely and expeditiously. Each in-country trainer personally carries medical textbooks for hand delivery to Black Lion Hospital library, a mandatory process known as the "Book Mule Program," described during cultural briefing sessions (Phillips, 2013).

Pursuing grants, project funding, donors, partners, and sponsors presents an ongoing but worthwhile challenge. Although we have been short-listed on a number of grants, we still have been operating with limited funds. In 2011 we received the British Medical Association Information Fund Grant, which provided an invaluable contribution toward shipment of current medical texts.

The Ethiopian government has completed building the new Central Medical Library. It incorporates collections of the Black Lion Hospital

FIGURE 1.2. Sandra Kendall teaching medical library literacy skills to residents of College of Health Sciences, 2012 (Credit: Carla Hagstrom)

FIGURE 1.3. Graduating class of librarians in front of AAU Library, 2011 (Credit: Carla Hagstrom)

library, the pharmacy library, and the nursing library. The existing medical library is roughly 8,000 square feet, but the new library is a six-story building of approximately 100,000 square feet. Obviously, many more books and library resources are required to fulfill the government's goal of a robust information environment for the health information needed by scientists, doctors, scholars, researchers, patients, and families.

To improve access to electronic resources for medical students and physicians at Black Lion Hospital, "the Ptolemy project was conceived in discussion between a surgeon and a librarian" (Beveridge, Howard, Burton, & Holder, 2003). The Ptolemy project is an extensive distance-learning opportunity for East African surgeons.

Membership in the Ptolemy project offers affiliated researchers an easily accessible portal providing quick links to relevant medical resources and access to UTL medical information e-resources. Registration for UTL e-resources is evaluated by a stringent review conducted by orthopedic surgeon Dr. Andrew Howard. In an article presenting the Ptolemy project as a scalable model, the author stated that "large university libraries have the technical capability to establish remote access at minimal extra cost. . . . From a technical perspective, therefore, expansion is straightforward" (Beveridge, 2003). The Ptolemy Library is a subset of UTL's electronic resources. Core resources selected by physicians for a variety of clinical specialties reside on the homepage of the website.

The authors envision that the Ptolemy Library would expand exponentially to meet specialty and subspecialty needs. Miliard Derbew, previous dean of medicine and one of the founders of the Ptolemy project, suggested that the original inclusion criteria established in 2001 be expanded to include TAAAC clinical partners in Ethiopia. UTL hosts the Ptolemy Library's website and the Mount Sinai Hospital library manages design and administrative work.

Clinical decision support resources not available through HINARI are made accessible via the Ptolemy Library. A value study of the Ptolemy Library was implemented during fall 2014. What we observed and hope to replicate is that access to UTL, one of the top three academic libraries in the American rankings (Donkin, 2012) will help clinicians in developing countries provide better patient care through exposure to leading evidence-based resources.

Sourcing full-text articles continues to be an ongoing challenge for physicians and medical students. The National Library of Medicine encourages use of their Loansome Doc service to fulfill this need. Several members of the Health Science Information Consortium of Toronto have agreed to partner with Black Lion Hospital library as their Loansome Doc ordering library. Participating libraries, selected for their specialty and subspecialty collections, include women's and infant health (Mount Sinai Hospital); pediatric health care (Hospital for Sick Children); trauma, emergency, and critical care (Sunnybrook Health Sciences Centre); and addiction and mental health (Centre for Addiction and Mental Health).

The most challenging of the deliverables has been the ability to conduct in-country training sessions. We agreed to deliver sessions introducing librarians, medical students, physicians, and allied health professionals to the breadth of available electronic resources, as well as evidence-based practices and the role of clinical librarianship, leadership, and management training for library staff.

In preparation for onsite training, a working team comprised of volunteers from the Health Science Information Consortium of Toronto created materials that could be distributed to participants and future trainers. The 2011 team of in-country trainers originated from this working team. Materials consisted of various formats such as print, CDs, DVDs, and online versions available via the TAAAC-LSP website. We are fortunate that, although Ethiopia has over eighty dialects, English is the language of instruction. As a governance guideline of TAAAC, trainers must secure professional and educational leave from their employers. Flights for trainers are reimbursed by UTL, and accommodations and in-country transport are provided by AAU College of Health Sciences.

The International Network for the Availability of Scientific Publications provided additional grant funding for our first training session. This permitted TAAAC-LSP to invite representatives from two additional Ethiopian university libraries, Jimma and Gondar. The second training session, conducted in 2012, continued to be funded by UTL and AAU. UTL also provided an honorarium for a presentation requested by a local church group interested in our global outreach. Further funds were raised by renting medical textbooks to a film production company.

As TAAAC-LSP project lead since 2008, I began with an initial medical library assessment at Black Lion Hospital library. I have since conducted a number of additional assessments for pharmacy and nursing, and completed four in-country training sessions and a number of distance learning sessions. TAAAC-LSP successfully shipped over 3,000 current, relevant medical textbooks to Black Lion Hospital library. My work has fostered the beginning of a fruitful, productive partnership in the transfer of knowledge and skills to librarians, medical librarians, nurses, physicians, and students of AAU's College of Health Sciences.

These endeavors revitalized my career precisely when I had begun questioning my continuing role as a librarian. My responsibilities as director of library services at Mount Sinai Hospital library have been enhanced by efforts to improve medical library services through access to electronic resources, introducing the role of the clinical librarian, and training in the application of best evidence and clinical decision support resources to my colleagues at AAU. Since our library is responsible for teaching medical students, the Black Lion Hospital library, as the fully affiliated teaching hospital for AAU, will position their medical library to promote the allied health information and learning needs of their students.

When Ethiopian coordinators were seeking educational partnerships to increase the number of master's and PhD graduates in the coming decade, they sought a medical librarian to attend their 2008 PhD symposium. I was the sole librarian at this international gathering of over 800 prospective partners. While being pulled in countless directions by numerous local faculties requesting access to library resources and services proved overwhelming, I also felt welcomed and appreciated.

During our first two-week training session in 2011, we introduced medical library literacy to over 140 participants, including 12 clinical residents. Training evaluations were positive. We continue to support librarian colleagues with posttraining email responses related to database searching and journal access. We advocated for a train-the-trainer model, recommending that the skills we taught would be shared with others in turn. A survey administered three months later indicated that sixteen librarians had themselves taught over 140 new learners. Although this is what we initially planned, we were still thrilled to achieve these results.

In our second session in 2012, over 250 participants attended, including 166 clinical residents from general surgery, orthopedic surgery, psychiatry, physiology, radiology, and emergency medicine. Upcoming training sessions already have a waiting list of clinical residents. Coteaching orthopedic surgical residents with Dr. Andrew Howard proved a great opportunity for TAAAC-LSP medical librarians. We expressed mutual respect for the different skills, knowledge, and expertise we each bring to patient care.

The most important takeaway from this project and any global health initiative is to understand that we should be committed to eliminating health inequities (Kidder, 2004). I am grateful for the opportunity to practice my professional competencies and knowledge as a medical librarian. Our work in Addis Ababa can be challenging, but is truly rewarding. In 2014 we focused our training on specialty and subspecialty clinicians and nurses while having Ethiopian librarians observe. Over 330 specialty clinicians attended these sessions. A new LCD projector and laptop will ensure that medical library colleagues continue to instruct on skills. We hope to establish a remote medical library "buddy" or partnering relationship, so we can continue to remotely assist.

TAAAC-LSP is not charitable work, since it is part of an educational university-to-university partnership. Ultimately, at the request of the Ethiopian government, we are attempting to build capacity by offering transfer of skills and knowledge to the top 3 percent of the country's educated population.

Performing global health work involves communicating your project as broadly as possible. As an annual update, the UTL chief librarian requires an evaluative review from TAAAC-LSP, which is shared with Health Science Information Consortium of Toronto members. We communicate challenges of this ongoing partnership via local, regional, national, and international poster presentations, oral presentations, interviews, and journal and newsletter articles. We presented a spring 2012 continuing education course for Ontario Health Libraries Association. Communication also extends to physicians, nurses, and allied health professionals interested in learning about medical library literacy that advances and supports practices in developing countries. All TAAAC-LSP media and publications are listed on our website (http://taaaclibrarygroup.wordpress.com/about_taaac_library_program/).

TAAAC-LSP has been invited to share our successes and challenges with other UofT global health projects. We provide trainers traveling to Ethiopia with materials and instructions and offer local sessions on library resources to groups or individuals. Scholars from developing countries are offered corresponding instruction when visiting UofT.

Anyone aspiring to establish a global library partnership would benefit from a checklist of common characteristics of a team leader: a sense of purpose, focus, persistence, and an unwavering desire to successfully complete deliverables. These characteristics, combined with creativity, resourcefulness, flexibility, strong listening skills, and a wicked sense of humor, should guarantee success. Always think bigger than you think can be possible. Stretch yourself, and have a great experience.

REFERENCES

Alem, A., Pain, C., Araya, M., & Hodges, B. D. (2010). Co-creating a psychiatric resident program with Ethiopians, for Ethiopians, in Ethiopia: The Toronto–Addis Ababa Psychiatry Project (TAAPP). *Academic Psychiatry, 34*(6), 424–432.

Beveridge, M., Howard, A., Burton, K., & Holder, W. (2003). The Ptolemy project: A scalable model for delivering health information in Africa. *BMJ, 327*(7418), 790–793.

Donkin, K. (2012, September 3). University of Toronto libraries third-best in American rankings. *Toronto Star*, p. GT4.

Phillips, C. (2013). Me? Ethiopia? The rewards of international collaboration. *Feliciter*, 59(3), 35–36.

Kidder, J. T. (2004). Mountains beyond mountains: The quest of Dr. Paul Farmer, a man who could cure the world. New York: Random House.

Unite for Sight. (n.d.) Cultural competency online course. Retrieved December 16, 2014, from http://www.uniteforsight.org/cultural-competency/.

Van Essen, C., Cartledge, P., Kyamanywa, P., & Manirakiza, A. (2012). Is HINARI appropriate for medical students in the developing world? *Tropical Medicine & International Health*, *17*(4), 406–408.

RECOMMENDED READING

Brook, S., Robertson, D., Makuwaza, T., & Hodges, B. D. (2010). Canadian residents teaching and learning psychiatry in Ethiopia: A grounded theory analysis focusing on their experiences. *Academic Psychiatry*, *34*(6), 433–437.

Cadotte, D. W., Blankstein, M., Bekele, A., Dessalegn, S., Pain, C., Derbew, M., & Howard, A. (2013). Establishing a surgical partnership between Addis Ababa, Ethiopia, and Toronto, Canada. *Canadian Journal of Surgery*, 56(3), E19.

Fekadu, A., & Thornicroft, G. (2014). Global mental health: Perspectives from Ethiopia. *Global Health Action*, *7*, 25, 447.

Fricchione, G. L., Borba, C. P., Alem, A., Shibre, T., Carney, J. R., & Henderson, D. C. (2012). Capacity building in global mental health: Professional training. *Harvard Review of Psychiatry*, *20*(1), 47–57.

Gathoni, N. (2012). Enhancing access to health information in Africa: A librarian's perspective. *Journal of Health Communication*, *17*(sup2), 18–22.

Kanyengo, C. W., Ajuwon, G. A., Kamau, N., Horta, C., & Anne, A. (2011). Knowledge and utilization of the United States National Library of Medicine's Biomedical Information Products and Services among African health sciences librarians. *Medical Reference Services Quarterly*, *30*(3), 257–268.

Kendall, S. (2010). From Toronto to East Africa: A medical library partnership. *JCHLA*, *31(3)*, 91–93.

Teshima, J. (2008). Teaching child psychiatry in Ethiopia: Challenges and rewards. *Journal of the Canadian Academy of Child and Adolescent Psychiatry*, *17*(3), 145.

CONNECTING WITH THE UNIVERSITY OF HONG KONG FOR PROGRAM AND PROFESSIONAL DEVELOPMENT

Lesley S. J. Farmer

Professional associations offer librarians opportunities to strengthen their competencies, including leadership, while building beneficial networks. These professional networks may range from specific librarianship interests to multitype library cooperation, and from local system groups to international organizations. Furthermore, professional organizations can link with other library entities such as librarian preparation programs to offer seamless professional development.

International professional library associations serve as a catalyst for international librarianship. In this instance, I will examine my partnership with the University of Hong Kong and its extensions, facilitated through participation in the International Association of School Librarianship (IASL), specifically in terms of information literacy.

As librarians work in cross-cultural settings, or with learners from different cultures, they should strive for cultural competence. Cultures are well-defined, sustained groups of people with common norms, expectations, and values, which can be distinguished from other culture groups. Thus, cultures might emerge from shared physical traits, interests, or attitudes: from Girl Scouts to knitters, from the Amish to terrorist cells (Cutler, 2005). In the globalized community, cultures are more likely to encounter one another, which can lead to misunderstandings and conflict due to inaccurate and preconceived attitudes (Hofstede, 1980). On the other hand, cultural interaction may result in increased tolerance and enriched knowledge (Nair, Norman, Tucker, & Burkert, 2012).

Cultural competence may be defined as a congruent set of knowledge, behaviors, and dispositions that enable one to work effectively in cross-cultural situations, interacting respectfully and valuing differences (National Association of Social Workers, 2001). It entails knowledge of other cultures, professional values of providing culturally competent service, fostering an atmosphere of inclusion, and encouraging proactive processes that increase diversity.

Cross-cultural competence begins with self-knowledge (Kalyanpur & Harry, 1999). Librarians need to examine their own cultural values, assumptions, expectations, and norms. Everyone has cultural prejudices, which color personal perceptions about the surrounding world. Identifying and owning up to these prejudices can help librarians do personal emotional work to improve their own mindsets, interact more authentically with their clientele, and avoid possible misunderstandings (Craig, 1996). These practices can help them understand how culture influences perspectives and strategize about means to change detrimental behavior and embrace difference.

In their 2012 diversity standards, the Association of College and Research Libraries identified behaviors of cross-cultural library leaders: sensitivity to and curiosity about other worldviews, cross-cultural knowledge and communication skills, support for a diverse workforce, and the ability to deal with ambiguity.

My partnership with Hong Kong followed a long and winding path. Rapaport (2008) asserted that participation in international programs can increase educators' repertoires of instructional strategies, expand their cultural sensitivity and perceptions, and influence their interpersonal relations in education. My own international education began in graduate school when I participated in a summer international exchange of social workers and youth leaders in France. After working as a professional librarian for a few years, I joined the Peace Corps, where I taught library science in Tunisia.

This experience motivated me to pursue a doctorate in adult education. My mentor recruited me to serve as an assistant editor for the IASL, which led to my attending and presenting at this organization. In 2004, then–vice president for association relations James Henri invited me to head the Information Literacy Special Interest Group. I developed site links to other information literacy resources and worked with IASL members to provide professional development.

Further, James Henri directed the Teacher Librarian Diploma Program at the University of Hong Kong (UHK). As coordinator of the California State University Long Beach Teacher Librarian program, I served in a counterpart position. Due to my professional expertise and experience with IASL, Henri asked me to serve as the UHK program's external evaluator, under the auspices of its School of Professional and Continuing Education (SPACE). This connection led to several projects and activities in Hong Kong.

Hong Kong's educational system reflects long occupation by the United Kingdom. The system is basically British in nature, and consists of six primary forms and seven secondary forms. Since its reversion to China, Hong Kong's curriculum has become more Chinese-oriented. The main strands of the curriculum include reading and literacy, science, technology, and moral education. Students must meet both English and Cantonese language requirements. The associate degree and diploma program usually require two years to complete, and the bachelor's program is set up as a three-year process. The master's degree typically requires an additional two-year commitment.

Under the direction of the Hong Kong Education and Manpower Bureau, every primary and secondary school is mandated to hire a qualified full-time teacher librarian. These teacher librarians need to be credentialed teachers and teacher librarians. In some cases, a classroom teacher takes the position for a year or two, but others find teacher librarianship to be their real niche. Much of their time is spent in collection management, but increasingly they work with teachers in reading promotion, information literacy, and technology competency efforts. Teacher librarians need to have a bachelor's degree, although most have already earned one for their first credential.

At one point, Education and Manpower Bureau in-house training provided the basis of academic preparation, but in 1999 a diploma program was established at UHK. UHK is the island's oldest institution of higher education, having begun in 1910 as a medical training center. Now it offers bachelor's through doctoral degrees in many subjects and serves almost 20,000 students. It offers Hong Kong's only master's degree in library and information management and its only diploma in the teacher librarian program.

In 1999, the diploma of teacher librarianship program consisted of ten modules with thirty-six credits total. For each module, classes were usually held weekly for eight to ten weeks, followed by the next module. Subjects included collection development and organization, technology, information sources and technology, information literacy, and collaboration. A field experience was built into each year's program. This approach blended theory and practice and stressed cataloging and instruction.

As external examiner of this program, I found the culminating tasks to be synthesizing readings, discussion, and site application. Although most classes were conducted face to face, all courses were mounted on UHK's interactive learning network, so students could retrieve presentations and readings online and post work digitally to the group. About eighty students were in the diploma program, and half that many were master's degree candidates. Most students worked full-time and travelled some distance to attend class, even though there are six instructional sites scattered throughout Hong Kong for the diploma program. To accommodate their needs further, courses tended to be held in the evenings and on Saturdays, and most documents were posted online. Several classes were outfitted with laptops for each student to facilitate interactive participation. Most full-time faculty were not native to Hong Kong (including Tasmania-born James Henri), though most part-time faculty were local teacher-librarian practitioners. Thus, library science students received a truly international education.

In reviewing the program, I thought that overall it prepared students for entrance-level teacher-librarian positions in Hong Kong primary and secondary schools. Both years provided a good mix of technical skills and foundational concepts. Having mentorship experiences in both years offered students and instructors a chance to benchmark their knowledge and skills in order to make timely adjustments. In a few modules, however, content did not adequately address current and future trends (the basis for ensuing course modifications). Management issues appeared to be the area with the greatest need for preparation.

I was required to visit the campus. Based on my preliminary report and prior library science teaching, I was asked by UHK to combine this visit with teaching that summer (2005) in their master's degree program in library and information management. I taught two courses in research methods and inquiry and initiated a collection management course. The students were all local residents, and ranged in age from early twenties to midfifties. Their interests and work settings reflected the full spectrum of librarianship: public, academic, school, and special. Courses ran for ten weeks, two evenings a week. Most students worked in libraries, and some had to travel two hours to attend class, making for extremely long days. In addition, I presented two professional development workshops for library science faculty.

In early August, 1999, IASL held its annual conference at UHK, the first time IASL had met in China. The local planning committee worked hard to make this conference special, down to the sequined conference bags. Given my SIG leadership skills, I was asked to help with last-minute preparations. This consisted largely of editing their program proceedings. Over 600 delegates from about thirty countries attended. At the opening meeting, Hong Kong teacher librarians and administrators were honored for their efforts, which drew much local attention. The conference was highlighted by children's performances and excellent food. Delegates had a chance to visit exemplary local school libraries. Over a hundred sessions addressed current issues of resources, instruction, collaboration, research, and technology. Even more learning occurred in hallways and at meals as teacher librarians from around the world shared their experiences.

Carol Kuhlthau, another active IASL member and an internationally known information literacy expert, arrived a week early to offer a professional development workshop for library science faculty. She and I also devised an information literacy workshop as a preconference offering. Not surprisingly, we had a full room for this interactive session.

I had received a research award from IASL on comparative preparation of teacher librarians. I was able to interview teacher librarians

FIGURE 2.1. IASL conference information literacy workshop (Credit: Lesley S. J. Farmer)

from around the world at the conference. The study was subsequently published in 2008 as a peer-reviewed chapter in *Educational Media and Technology Annual*.

The Hong Kong visit also established the foundation for a coauthored book on information literacy assessment. James Henri suggested writing this volume together. Three months in Hong Kong provided extensive opportunities for us to discuss possible content and strategy and draft sections of the book. UHK has a sizeable library collection, so I was able to cull it for sources not available at my home campus.

Prior IASL activities, as well as related professional work and international travel, prepared me for success. Certainly experiencing a different culture while sharing common values of librarianship provided a rich learning environment. My experience was both fascinating and challenging. Because I was teaching as a paid professor, I needed to obtain a work visa, which required extensive documentation. I had to list my family background, as did my Hong Kong sponsor, along with transcripts and letters of recommendation. Once I arrived in Hong Kong, I needed to open a local bank account and set up university details such as keys, office, and meal plans. Even transportation was something I had to negotiate from scratch, since I was not welcomed on arrival or given much guidance when starting work.

I tried to learn a few Cantonese expressions before arriving, and printed out pages of phrases, but I was not understood when I spoke these words. Locals answered in English. Fortunately, most public areas had signs in English and kanji, so I navigated well. I ran into language problems only when I observed an off-campus class, because that neighborhood had limited tourist traffic.

On a positive note, the rest of the faculty accepted me as an equal—and local—teacher, and let me have full control of the course and teaching duties. On the other hand, only one of them, a kind Chinese American female, showed me around the area. Later in the summer, another visiting teacher from New Zealand arrived and we did a bit of tourist activity together. Even though my sponsoring colleague stayed in the same faculty residence, we seldom ate together, and he did not set up my worksite details, and no faculty visited my classes or asked me about American library science education.

The SPACE director discussed administration with me, and introduced me to influential local librarians, including one who showed me the impressive main public library. On my part, I asked extensively about Hong Kong education, observed UHK library science classes, and visited local school libraries. Hong Kong had more religious-affiliated libraries

FIGURE 2.2. Hong Kong's central public library (Credit: Lesley S. J. Farmer)

than I expected, and some of the settings were interesting, including a newspaper library, a women's club recreational library, and several private universities and schools.

My conversations with James Henri about information literacy and assessment were thought-provoking and enriching, even though we made little writing headway that summer. The library was a fine source of learning, and I read extensively from its collection. Several librarians provided inside perspectives about Hong Kong professional experience, as well as insights about local information literacy instruction.

My main joy was the students: eager, hard-working, and appreciative learners. Their English was surprisingly good, though they tended to downplay their abilities. They stated that they were accustomed to lecture methods of instruction and were not used to class discussion, which echoed the research findings of Zhang (2000). Nevertheless, they came to enjoy and participate enthusiastically in class interaction. By the end of the course, students were comfortable sharing critical analysis and independent viewpoints. I had them undertake more service-learning than they had previously experienced, and they had to write more than usual. I also gave them timely, specific feedback, which guided their work and facilitated learning. They were not accustomed to this approach, but greatly appreciated it. On the last day, they hugged me, gave me presents, and sincerely wanted me to stay or return to teach them more. A few continued their correspondence, and some are still Facebook friends.

On a personal note, I had never been away from my family for such a long time. However, I had good Internet connectivity, so I corresponded with them daily. International phone calls from Hong Kong are surprisingly inexpensive, so we conducted weekly calls. Midway during the summer, my husband and son visited me in Hong Kong for a week.

As a result of my work, the UHK teacher-librarian and library science programs changed. The Teacher Librarian Diploma Program

FIGURE 2.3. University of Hong Kong students in class computer lab (Credit: Lesley S. J. Farmer)

introduced management courses and strengthened their technology and instructional courses. The master's program continues to offer the collection development course.

Unfortunately, my main contacts at UHK changed jobs—and countries—and one retired. While a number of us keep in contact occasionally, we have not worked on projects together since 2005 except for presenting at some virtual conferences developed by two UHK library science faculty. Sustaining efforts at long distance is challenging, particularly if individual professional agendas change. Moreover, my colleagues stopped being active in IASL, so professional networking was less supported.

I am not certain who learned more in my instructional role, Hong Kong students or myself—probably the latter. I encourage more library educators to cross-fertilize their profession. Back home at California State University Long Beach (CSULB), I shared my experience with my students through photographs and information gleaned from the IASL conference at UHK. I also had my UHK and CSULB colleagues exchange their perspectives and practices about teacher librarianship. I presented my experiences at a CSULB librarianship program gala and a conference of the California School Library Association. Further, I developed a comparative school librarianship course, which was awarded funding. The course includes an option for students to attend the IASL conference in Moscow.

My travel experiences gave me more sensitivity to visiting scholars' situations, as predicted by Rapaport (2008). I presented a session about sponsoring visiting scholars at a conference of the Association of Library and Information Science Educators. I initiated a visiting scholars program sponsored by the Goethe Institute. Locally, I joined the CSULB International Committee and have contributed to documents about visiting scholar programs.

Professionally, on the national and international levels, I was elected IASL vice president of association relations, with the support of Hong Kong and affiliated votes. This position has led to other international initiatives and partnerships, which continue to inform my students and myself. I also helped establish an international task force within the American Association of School Librarians, and founded the international subcommittee for the Media Specialist SIG of International Society for Technology in Education.

I serve on a joint committee between IASL and the International Federation of Library Associations, which has developed satellite meetings to which I have given presentations. We are developing advocacy training, for which I wrote the manual. My continued work in IASL led to a Fulbright experience in Brazil, collaboration with school library associations in Nepal, and my editing a book on library services for youth in Japan, Russia, and the United States.

I have discovered that an intercultural skill set should include mutual academic domain knowledge and practice, mutual professional values, flexibility and openness, active listening skills, negotiation skills, politeness and patience, resourcefulness, dependability, authentic interest in and care for clientele, and research and interviewing skills. Those who present, and especially those who teach abroad, need to be self-sufficient. International experiences, even if challenging, should be sought and leveraged to gain knowledge about librarianship perspectives and practices in other cultures, and to understand the extent to which implementation of school library programs is culturally defined. Such learning helps librarians more effectively serve a diverse clientele.

Lastly, I acknowledge the significance of professional associations as the major means of continuing professional development, networking, and initiatives that can have international impact and sustainability. It is amazing to observe the universality of school librarianship values, and to understand how those values are culturally contextualized in daily operations. Librarians need to be aware of the social dynamics of information literacy. They should serve as change agents, providing appropriate leadership via cross-cultural professional development, communities of practice, and educational reform efforts. Supporting these efforts requires initiative, professional expertise, and networking skills sustained over time.

Moreover, librarians need to instruct preservice librarians and mentor emerging professionals both locally and abroad. They should encourage new librarians to become involved in international professional associations and provide leadership opportunities to sustain and improve them, thereby furthering these educational dialogues and actions.

REFERENCES

Association of College and Research Libraries. (2012). *Diversity standards: Cultural competency of academic libraries*. Chicago: American Library Association.

Craig, R. L. (1996). *The ASTD training and development handbook: A guide to human resource development*. New York: McGraw-Hill.

Cutler, J. (2005). The cross-cultural communication trainer's manual. Aldershot, UK: Gower Publishing.

Hofstede, G. (1984). *Culture's consequences: International differences in work-related Values*, Vol. 5. Thousand Oaks, CA: Sage.

Kalyanpur, M., & Harry, B. (1999). *Culture in special education: Building reciprocal family-professional relationships*. Baltimore, MD: PH Brookes Pub.

Nair, I., Norman, M., Tucker, R. G., & Burkert, A. (2012). The challenge for global literacy: An ideal opportunity for liberal professional education. *Liberal Education*, 98(1), 56–61.

National Association of Social Workers. (2001). *Standards for cultural competence in social work practice*. Washington, DC: National Association of Social Workers.

Rapoport, A. (2008). The impact of international programs on pedagogical practices of their participants: A Russian experience. *Teachers and Teaching: Theory and Practice*, *14*(3), 225–238.

Zhang, L. F. (2000). University students' learning approaches in three cultures: An investigation of Biggs's 3P model. *The Journal of Psychology*, *134*(1), 37–55.

RECOMMENDED READING

Biggs, J. B. (1978). Individual and group differences in study processes. *British Journal of Educational Psychology*, 48(3), 266–279.

Dorner, D. G., & Gorman, G. E. (2006). Information literacy education in Asian developing countries: Cultural factors affecting curriculum development and programme delivery. *IFLA Journal*, *32*(4), 281–293.

Edmundson, A. (Ed.). (2006). *Globalized e-learning cultural challenges*. Hershey, PA: IGI Global.

Laroche, L. (2012). *Managing cultural diversity in technical professions*. Florence, KY: Routledge.

Lau, J. (Ed.). (2008). *Information literacy: International perspectives*. Munich, Germany: K. G. Saur.

Liaw, M. L. (2006). E-learning and the development of intercultural competence. *Language Learning & Technology*, *10*(3), 49–64.

McMahon, C. A., & Bruce, C. S. (2002). Information literacy needs of local staff in cross-cultural development projects. *Journal of International Development*, *14*(1), 113–127.

Sheets, R. (2004). *Diversity pedagogy*. Boston: Allyn & Bacon.

Smith, C. (2006). Multiple cultures, multiple intelligences: Applying cognitive theory to usability of digital libraries. *Libri*, 56(4), 227–238.

THE CUNY-SHANGHAI LIBRARY FACULTY EXCHANGE PROGRAM

Participants Remember, Reflect, and Reshape

Sheau-yueh J. Chao, Beth Evans, Ryan Phillips,
Mark Aaron Polger, Beth Posner, Ellen Sexton

This chapter recounts the outcomes and experiences of six American librarians who participated in an international librarian exchange program that ran from spring 2010 through fall 2011. The exchange brought together the City University of New York (CUNY) and two universities in Shanghai, China: Shanghai University (SU) and Shanghai Normal University (SNU). The program was inspired, in part, by recognition of the diversity of CUNY's student body and growing awareness of the increasing globalization of information and education. For the Chinese librarians, the exchange offered an opportunity to learn from the West and showcase their own innovations. The traveling participants—eight librarians from six of the CUNY colleges and six librarians from SU and SNU—benefited from individual opportunities for learning and the collective development of new visions for academic library services.

HIGHER EDUCATION AND EXCHANGES IN CHINA: A BRIEF REVIEW

From the time Mao Zedong and the Communists assumed power in 1949 through the late 1990s, sociopolitical status constituted the primary criteria for admission to college in China. The re-institution of the college entrance examination (*gaokao*) in 1997 expanded access to higher education (Liu, 2012). Enrollment quotas were removed and the student population exploded. The number of young people attending college in China jumped from 1.08 million students in 1998 to 20 million in 2004 (Zha, 2011), and reached 23 million students in 2011 (National Bureau of Statistics of China, 2012). As more students gained access to higher education, the structure of the institutions and the nature of support began to change. Colleges and universities were no longer centrally controlled by the state, many institutions of higher learning were consolidated, specific universities were chosen for additional funding with the aim of achieving and maintaining world-class status, institutions now had the freedom to borrow money from commercial lenders, and colleges and universities began to charge tuition (Li, Whalley, Zhang, & Zhao, 2011; Hewitt, 2008).

Because of the strong desire of so many Chinese to attend college and the opening up of seats in institutions of higher education, China now faces high levels of unemployment among college graduates (Wang, 2011; Wangshu, 2012). In addition,

> [T]he Chinese authorities recognize the need for curricular and pedagogical reform in [higher] education, to ensure that graduates have the knowledge and skills that the modernizing economy requires. In particular, there is recognition of the need for [higher] education generically to develop skills of critical inquiry, creativity, problem solving, communication and team work. (OECD, 2009, p. 11)

As higher education has grown in China, so has the number of students and faculty participating in international exchanges. Many Western universities send students on short study abroad or semester- or year-long programs at Chinese universities. And many thousands of Chinese students travel abroad for education each year. Close to 700 transnational partnerships, where students study in one country but receive their degrees from another, had been approved by the Chinese government in 2004, but unapproved programs also exist (Yang, 2008). An increasing number of Western universities have established campuses in China (Hewitt, 2008), and librarian exchanges involving Western public and academic libraries have been occurring for quite some time (Scherlen, Shao, & Cramer, 2009; Johnson, Shi, & Shao, 2010; Stueart, 1987; Williams, 2000).

CUNY-SHANGHAI EXCHANGE EXPERIENCES: PARTICIPANTS AND SETTINGS

All three universities involved in the CUNY-Shanghai Exchange—CUNY, SU, and SNU—are public institutions situated in dense, urban settings. CUNY was established to educate New Yorkers and others as an integrated system dedicated to affording access to academic excellence. CUNY has twenty-eight libraries spread across twenty-four distinct colleges, with its librarians regularly working together to achieve common goals. Their collaboration has resulted in a shared union catalog, consortial licensing of electronic databases, and professional development across campuses, among other combined efforts. The Chinese host institutions both have multiple campuses situated in the downtown areas of the city and also in the distant suburbs. The newer suburban campuses were built to provide more space for students, faculty, and staff, as well as to house facilities and resources.

Shanghai itself is an incredibly fast-growing city, expanding outward and upward. Its population far exceeds that of New York City, and its many monumental new buildings are designed to impress. With a continually growing public transportation system and more people arriving each day to seek opportunities, the growth of this metropolis is so fast-paced that even online maps quickly prove to be out-of-date. A sense of the overwhelming size and pace of the city of Shanghai offered a valuable perspective to seasoned New York City librarians as they returned home to assist CUNY library patrons.

CUNY librarians each spent four weeks in Shanghai comparing and contrasting library services. Each focused on a service area, such as reference, interlibrary loan, instruction, or cataloging. The goal was to learn as much as time would allow. The following reflections document how their experiences allowed them to evolve in their work and contribute to the goals of their individual colleges and libraries, as well as to the general mission of CUNY.

By touring and observing the daily functions of Chinese academic libraries, none of the CUNY librarians were attempting to "fix" or "change" either their system or that of their partners. Nor did they assume the role of Alexis de Tocqueville, who visited North America and reported to France, or as United Nations observers sent to a warring region to assess the propriety of foreign operations. Instead, they endeavored to consider how libraries in one of the fastest-growing countries on earth conduct library services. There was no prior belief that

Chinese or American librarians are more successful in their respective approaches. Rather, CUNY librarians set out with the mindset of explorers, knowing little about what to expect, but seeking to learn and build a foundation for moving forward individually and collectively within CUNY and the world.

LIBRARY AND DEPARTMENT TOURS

In Shanghai, participants enjoyed extensive tours of the host libraries, focusing on overall library operations, the functions of individual library departments, course offerings, budgets, personnel, circulation, access services, acquisitions, collection management, technical services, and cataloging. Although language barriers and schedules did impose limits, working within one institution with several campus libraries allowed for extended discussion and queries. Time spent in specific library units and departments of the host libraries fostered a more in-depth understanding of daily operations of academic libraries.

CUNY participants also visited many other university libraries—including those at Tongji, Fudan, Jiao Tong, and East China Normal—to meet with even more librarians, library administrators, and staff. The value of these tours lay in developing a more generalized understanding of Chinese libraries. All the libraries visited were large, even magnificent. The belief held by many Western librarians that a library is the heart of a university is evident in the shape of the SU main campus library—an open book—and its location at the center of the campus. Public libraries in China proved to be equally impressive. The main Shanghai Public Library, which holds the largest genealogical collection and family history records in China, and the recently built Pudong District Library are two stellar examples. Some participants toured libraries beyond Shanghai, visiting those at Beijing and Nanjing Universities.

In Chinese libraries a great deal of thought, energy, and resources are dedicated to the scale and size of library buildings, staff, numbers of books purchased, and funds dedicated to electronic resources. The numbers in aggregate are used to illustrate the effectiveness of library operations. Libraries in the United States also concentrate on metrics of quantity through ACRL reference statistics or return-on-investment figures that, in turn, demonstrate effectiveness. Yet the value that librarians contribute to the mission of universities and their patrons cannot be captured solely by these measurements. In essence, all that librarians do to address patron needs contributes to learning and research. One outcome of this exchange, and all others like it, lies in the ongoing professional development of librarians.

In general—due to cultural differences, lack of familiarity with host viewpoints, and language barriers that made for awkward communication—specific recommendations were avoided and criticism moderated to cultivate an open and collegial atmosphere. However, Janey Chao, the only CUNY librarian fluent in Mandarin, and thus in the best position to make confident assessments, did draw up recommendations. These included allocating more space for study room areas at SU Library, giving more attention to student concerns and responses, increasing the hours the circulation desk is open, promoting services to teaching departments, reviewing the administrative structure of library departments, and providing better subject access to the library online catalog.

PROFESSIONAL PRESENTATIONS

Each of the six visiting librarians was responsible for some formal student instruction and professional development presentations to library staff on topics such as digital collections, subject librarianship, the liaison librarian model, business information in the United States, electronic resources, Serials Solutions, SFX (link-resolving software), institutional repositories, and digital media collections.

Those hosted at SU planned and presented eight lectures each to new library professionals and students majoring in library science. Each class lasted several hours, allowing time for presentations and general discussion. Topics were chosen in light of each librarian's expertise as well as the interests of library school faculty and class attendees, who explained that much of their education focuses more on technology than service. They were interested in digital information as well as user needs and services. The visiting librarians shared PowerPoint slides so the class could refer to them, and while interactions were mostly in class, at least some students also emailed and met with participants outside of class.

All lectured on CUNY and their home colleges. Chao taught about cooperative cataloging and outsourcing, e-reserves, SFX, FRBR and RDA, information literacy, acquisitions, subject specialists, outreach, archives, rare books, and digital collections. Beth Posner was assigned topics reflecting her work as a library resource-sharing specialist, as well as patron-driven acquisitions, the impact of interlibrary loan services on periodical acquisitions and licensing, the state of ILL and cooperative collection development and purchasing, cloud storage and procurement of print and digital materials, embedded librarianship, and the popularity of academic libraries.

Mark Aaron Polger taught classes about marketing, public relations and outreach, faculty status for librarians, and his role as an instruction and reference librarian. Drawing on his previous work as a medical librarian in Canada, he lectured on health sciences librarianship in hospital and library settings. Ellen Sexton presented on issues in U.S. academic libraries, technical and public services, serials librarianship and scholarly communication, information literacy, libraries as physical spaces, digital libraries, and library assessment.

After the official lectures, fruitful discussions often continued. Chinese students were interested in library school education in the United States, and the creativity and user-centricity of American library service. The liveliest participation sparked in Posner's class occurred while looking at a map of China, where everyone pointed out and spoke about their hometowns. This activity allowed everyone to get to know each other, learn about China, and share memories, personal stories, and hometown pride while practicing English. The most amusing conversations concerned stereotyping, whether unfair, such as that no American can do even the simplest math, or arguably true, such as that Chinese is a much more difficult language to learn than English.

COMPARATIVE LIBRARIANSHIP

As the program evolved, participants experienced a nuanced understanding of the role of academic libraries and librarians in China and the United States. Learning from Shanghai colleagues about their responsibilities, work, goals, and aspirations informed the professional acumen of the CUNY librarians and solidified their understanding of the value of librarians. The word for librarian in Mandarin is 图书馆员, pronounced *tú shū guǎn yuán*. The meaning directly refers to any library employee who manages the work of a library, whether their tasks are clerical or professional in scope.

Many Chinese librarians who perform work similar to that of U.S. librarians do not hold an MLS degree. Their subject background is often considered to be more important than a library science degree. This emphasis could be of interest to smaller libraries in the West, which, conversely, are often not in a position to hire subject bibliographers or selectors with a background in the disciplines they cover, but which insist that the librarian have an MLS degree.

Librarians often discuss their professional identity and how perceptions of librarians affect the work they perform with patrons. They even question what to call themselves within the context of a rapidly changing information environment—librarian, information scientist, or something else. As we observed the different roles librarians play in the

United States and China, it became evident that the term "librarian" is only as limiting as each library and librarian allows. While titles help professionals align themselves and reach consensus with regard to professional responsibilities, it was clear from observing Chinese librarians that it is more important how librarians translate their skills and knowledge to build processes and services to effectively meet patron needs.

As for specific library functions in China, several differences were observable. SNU supports an active in-house software development unit, reminiscent of the merging of information technology and traditional library functions seen in many U.S. libraries. However, SNU also supports a novelty research department, which scouts out topics of interest for faculty to ensure that this research has not been done before. This level of service is not typical for an American academic library, but it is a hallmark of a Chinese research library.

Reference and reader services in Chinese libraries seemed similar, but on closer examination, the service models differ. Although Chinese librarians are concerned foremost with keeping order in their reading rooms, where many students take advantage of a quiet space to work, U.S. librarians focus more on working with students to teach or identify the best resources for research. In another example, Posner introduced tools, such as the Rethinking Resource Sharing Initiative's *Manifesto for Resource Sharing* and the *STAR Checklist for Best Practices in Resource Sharing*, to Shanghai librarians in hope of sparking discussion about their applicability to information resource–sharing needs and practices in China.

CHALLENGES OF COMMUNICATION: LANGUAGE AND CENSORSHIP

CUNY participants were chosen specifically because of their specializations and personal characteristics, such as flexibility and respectfulness, which were believed to be more important than their actual Chinese language skills. Only one CUNY librarian could speak Mandarin fluently, but all of the Shanghai librarians who came to CUNY could speak English. Many librarians in Shanghai did not speak English or were uncomfortable speaking it. While overcoming language obstacles can be a challenging and even enjoyable aspect of a foreign visit, it is deeply humbling and frustrating when lack of language skills prevents potentially rewarding in-depth conversations with foreign colleagues.

Chao, CUNY's only native Chinese speaker, notes disadvantages as well as advantages of knowing a host country's language. Born and raised in Taiwan, her instruction and presentations were presented in bilingual format. Although her library school lectures were offered in English, she encouraged students to ask questions in either English or Chinese. Bilingual handouts were distributed, which contained ready references for future use. Responses from students were strong and positive about these new learning experiences. One drawback of being a native Chinese speaker, however, was that most of her travels and library visits were conducted without a guide, since the host institution probably assumed she didn't need additional assistance.

Other participants' library school lectures were delivered in English, without translators. It was unclear how much was understood, especially since many students were shy or unaccustomed to speaking in English. Thus, communication was challenging, and second-guessing what should and should not be said was a constant issue. It was also interesting to observe different ways of information sharing in the libraries, such as at SU, where there were regular announcements on campus loudspeakers, ongoing activities held among library staff such as participating in the campus's Chrysanthemum Festival, and at SNU where there was a scrolling suggestion area on the library's homepage.

Even more challenging was the issue of access to information in China, a core value for U.S. librarians. The American Library Association Bill of Rights states, "Libraries should challenge censorship in the fulfillment of their responsibility to provide information and enlightenment." And although participants sought technological fixes to break through the "Great Firewall of China" through VPNs and proxy software, it did not seem appropriate to directly challenge censorship in public arenas. Despite the interest in attitudes toward censorship and information sharing in China, there was a reluctance to engage colleagues in sensitive topics because of a (possibly unjustified) fear of unknown future social-political ramifications. When broached, however, such as during an impromptu group discussion about Google's move to using Hong Kong servers, diverging opinions were revealed. An older Chinese librarian insisted that students could access all they needed from library databases, but a more recent graduate invoked Orwell's *1984*.

For example, Polger found himself self-censoring during his classes and while interacting with students and fellow librarians. Although students were curious about social and political life in North America, he was hesitant to discuss topics such as rallies, protests, and First Amendment rights. When discussing access to news, he avoided mentioning Facebook or Twitter as sources because they are not available in China. Some students, sensing his hesitation, emphasized that China has its own Facebook (*Renren*) and Twitter (*Sina Weibo*).

Polger was deeply concerned that censorship might oppress students. In his classes, he demonstrated that academic libraries in China and the United States both subscribe to EBSCO databases, but he did not discuss with students whether citations were flagged and omitted based on controversial content. He quickly bypassed topics that might bring up questions and debate. Polger believed he was doing an injustice by censoring his teaching. However, he was reassured by his supervisor at SU that Chinese citizens are happy living in a Communist country. Outside the classroom, Polger realized he could not be completely open with colleagues. Unaware that he should not have brought up any of the "3 Ts"—Tibet, Taiwan, and Tiananmen Square—he did, and found that most of the group either kept silent or quickly changed topics.

CHALLENGES OF PROGRAM DESIGN

This particular exchange program was designed to last just two years, with back-to-back exchanges meant to strengthen bonds and build on each other. However, by the time one of the last two CUNY participants arrived in China, she sensed that her hosts had possibly become accustomed to American visitors. Posner, the fourth CUNY librarian to visit SU in only two years, believed she was seen as just another CUNY representative, rather than someone with unique perspectives to share. The Chinese had already heard all about CUNY, and although she was from another campus with a focus on serving graduate students, she was not asked much about either this or her interlibrary loan work. This was probably because most librarians are not directly involved with interlibrary loan, and those who enjoy use of an established service within China have less need for the extended services provided by many U.S. academic libraries.

Another interesting aspect of designing an international exchange program is the logistics of housing, meals, and similar concerns. Several participants needed to find vegetarian food in China, but it was difficult to locate. And, while SNU participants stayed in an on-campus hotel, SU visitors were housed in the International Student Dormitory, which allowed them to meet more students and have an enriched daily experience.

Many details of program design must be left to another venue, but it should be stated that beyond the basic challenges of financially supporting an international exchange program, a myriad of institutional, technological, physical, legal, political, administrative, human-related, and knowledge-based impediments to future international collaborations exist and must be acknowledged. While the goal of exposing fourteen

CUNY, SNU, and SU librarians to services at libraries in major urban centers across the world was met, additional outcomes must be realized to ensure ongoing financial support. Program support also requires time, design, and planning, with input from those involved on both sides of the exchange. Further, contact with developers of and participants in other international librarian exchange programs should be undertaken to share lessons learned and improve future experiences for all.

PROGRAM SUCCESSES

From the point of view of CUNY participants and administrators, outcomes and accomplishments included learning about library practices in Chinese educational institutions and exploring how and why policies, procedures, and services in U.S. and Chinese academic libraries work and how they might be improved. Opportunities for ongoing professional discussions about resource sharing and other library practices and philosophies, as well as collaboration on research and writing projects, have also been identified.

For many CUNY library faculty, interest in participating in this exchange was prompted by their work with the university's ethnically diverse student body. Eighteen percent of CUNY students identify as Asian or Pacific Islanders, according to the CUNY Office of Institutional Research. At Baruch College, where Ryan Phillips and Chao work, 38.6 percent identify as Asian. Following the exchange, Phillips sought ways to connect with this constituency, including becoming a track leader in a program, the Global Finance and Economics Baruch Leadership Academy, designed to attract high school students from around the world to his college.

Posner's experience as a newcomer to a university in another country gave her a profound sense of the challenges all international students navigate. She now consciously seeks them out to assist them at the reference desk and beyond, suggesting that librarians join their networks. She offers individual and group meetings as well as basic instructional handouts in popular languages. Now that Posner has direct contacts in China, they can help her access Chinese language material needed by CUNY patrons. Despite improvements in the discovery, availability, and delivery of information, challenges remain in accessing information from around the world, including copyright and licensing terms and limitations in staffing, procedures, and policy. However, the need for global information to address shared problems, as well as for individual education and development, is more important than ever.

After identifying the need for more marketing and promotion of library services in the Chinese libraries he visited, as well as intelligent purposing of library space, Polger has been inspired to focus on space and promotion in his home library. Ellen Sexton's residency prompted her to compile a bibliography of English language sources on the criminal justice system in China. This supplements her work with specialized criminal justice collections, and should be of particular interest to her colleagues, as her campus is currently exploring partnership opportunities with criminal justice educational institutions in China.

Beth Evans recommends use of an online forum to merge student book discussion groups in Shanghai and New York. By linking the freshman Common Reading program at Brooklyn College to Shanghai Normal University Library Readers Association, Chinese students eager to improve their English would be given opportunities to discuss their reading in English with American students. Both groups could broaden their conversations to include a more diverse set of interpretations. Similarly, international student clubs such as Students in Free Enterprise, which already operates at both SNU and Brooklyn, could collaborate on effective proposals to create economic development in their respective surrounding communities.

Chao brought back an assignment requested by the director of Shanghai University Library to revise the English version of the library's homepage and Handbook on Library Services. Baruch's library has communicated with SNU about the prospect of cross-training professional development, shared user and reference services, library education, staff training, and technical assistance via electronic conference or webinars. Chao also continues to participate in the International Conference of Institutes and Libraries for Chinese Overseas Studies, which focuses on international resource sharing and library cooperation among Chinese overseas studies programs.

Moreover, Evans proposes a joint research project with an SNU librarian to determine whether there is any relationship across the two cultures between career choice, preprofessional education, and the desire and opportunity to continue one's education in the library field after job placement. Simultaneously, they will investigate possibilities for shared continuing education, professional development, and conference attendance and presentations. Posner has also been in contact with Chinese colleagues about developing presentation proposals.

Evans, working with the International Relations Round Table of the Library Association of CUNY, in conjunction with the Chinese American Library Association, organized an open discussion and panel focusing on the education of Chinese librarians. The program featured Teng (Tony) Cheng, a librarian who had acted as a guide and translator for CUNY librarians hosted at SNU, who visited the State University of New York Stony Brook Health Sciences Library in the summer of 2013.

Therefore, many useful starting points for discussion have been identified: from staffing, library education, training, user services, use of library space, reference, instruction and course-related lectures, to challenges associated with growing interest in library collaboration and resource sharing. As Chao declares, "By building relationships across borders with our fellow librarians, we open dialogue of shared concerns and strategies for future development and promotion of librarianship locally, regionally, and globally."

CONCLUSIONS

Whether through take-home lessons or future collaboration, the significance of librarian exchange programs such as this will ultimately be measured by the development of quality library services, awareness of the latest developments in the library profession, and commitment to building and maintaining state-of-the-art academic libraries and library services in the world's largest metropolitan areas. Although this exchange program concluded after only two exploratory years, there are hopes that it will be reinstated someday. A variety of connections are possible between academic libraries and librarians working thousands of miles apart. It is encouraging that librarians from both Shanghai and New York are enthusiastic not only about developing future faculty exchanges, but about working together on information literacy courses, new technologies for library services, information commons, chat and email reference, and faculty publications. The value of an international library exchange program can extend well beyond the individual and positively shape services for patrons by librarians, globally, now and in the future.

REFERENCES AND RECOMMENDED READING

At CUNY, a library faculty exchange with Shanghai. (June 2, 2010). *CUNY Library News*. Retrieved from http://www1.cuny.edu/mu/library-news/2010/06/02/at-cuny-a-library-faculty-exchange-with-shanghai/.

Chen, S., & Liu, J. (2005). Using libraries in China. Know before you go. *College & Research Libraries News*, 66(2), 124–130.

City University of New York. (2012). *Investing in our future: The City University of New York's 2012–2016 Master Plan*. Retrieved from http://www.cuny.edu/news/publications/masterplan.pdf.

College of Staten Island. (2012). *The Center for International Service: The CUNY China Program*. Retrieved from http://www.csi.cuny.edu/international/china_programs.html.

CUNY initiates exchange programs with Chinese university libraries. (November 9, 2009). *CUNY Library News*. Retrieved from http://www1.cuny.edu/mu/library-news/2009/11/09/cuny-initiates-exchange-program-with-chinese-university-libraries/.

Gallagher, M., Hasan, A., Canning, M., Newby, H., Saner-Yiu, L., & Whitman, I. (2009). *OECD reviews of tertiary education: China*. Retrieved from http://www.oecd.org/education/skills-beyond-school/42286617.pdf.

Gashurov, I. (2010). Academic library exchange: Shanghai, China and New York City. *International Leads*, *24*(3), 5–8.

Han, S. (2000). Shanghai between state and market in urban transformation. *Urban Studies*, *37*, 2091–2112.

Johnson, M., Shi, W., & Shao, X. (2010). Exploring library service models at Fudan University and Appalachian State University: Experiences from an International Librarian Exchange program. *International Information & Library Review*, *42*(3), 186–194.

Kelsey, P., & Kelsey, S. (2003). *Outreach services in academic and special libraries*. Binghamton, NY: Haworth Information Press.

Li, Y., Whalley, J., Zhang, S., & Zhao, X. (2011). The higher educational transformation of China and its global implications. *The World Economy*, *34*, 516–545.

Liu, L. (2012). An overview of development of higher education access in China. *Higher Education Studies*, *2*(2), 107–113.

National Bureau of Statistics of China. (February 22, 2012). *Statistical communiqué of the People's Republic of China on the 2100 national economic and social development*. Retrieved from http://www.stats.gov.cn/nglish/newsandcomingevents/t20120222_402786587.htm.

Scherlen, A., Shao, X., & Cramer, E. (2009). Bridges to China: Developing partnerships between serials librarians in the United States and China. *Serials Review*, *35*(2), 75–79.

Stueart, R. D. (1987). US-China library exchange growing rapidly. *International Leads*, *1*(1): 3.

Turvey, J. (2012). The CUNY-Shanghai Library Faculty Exchange Program. *CALA Occasional Paper Series*, (11), 1–5.

Wang, X., & Liu, J. (2011). China's higher education expansion and the task of economic revitalization. *Higher Education*, *62*, 213–229.

Wangshu, L. (July 17, 2012). Graduate degrees no guarantee for jobs. *China Daily*. Retrieved from http://www.chinadailyapac.com/article/graduate-degrees-no-guarantee-jobs.

Williams, B. (2000). Fujian adventure: Final report. *OLA Quarterly*, 6(4), 11–13.

Winston, M. (1999). *Managing multiculturalism and diversity in the library: Principles and issues for administrators*. New York: Haworth Press.

Wu, J., & Huang, R. (2003). The academic library development in China. *Journal of Academic Librarianship*, 29(4), 249–253.

Yang, R. (2008). Transnational higher education in China: Contexts, characteristics and concerns. *Australian Journal of Education*, 52(3), 272–286.

Yi, L. (2011). Auditing Chinese higher education? The perspectives of returnee scholars in an elite university. *International Journal of Educational Development*, *31*, 505–514.

Zha, Q. (2011). China's move to mass higher education in a comparative perspective. *Compare*, *41*(6), 751–768.

FULBRIGHT EXPERIENCES

TRANSCENDING ETHNIC, RACIAL, AND POLITICAL CONFLICT TO ACHIEVE UNDERSTANDING BETWEEN THE GREEK AND TURKISH CYPRIOT LIBRARY COMMUNITIES

Constantia Constantinou

Cultivating relationships and friendships among different ethnic, racial, and politically diverse societies is a perpetual endeavor, especially when conflict among these groups has been rooted for centuries in peoples' minds and character. This essay describes my work as a Fulbright Senior Specialist in 2005 and as Fulbright Scholar in 2011 in Cyprus. The Fulbright Program is sponsored by the United States Department of State, Bureau of Educational and Cultural Affairs. Under a cooperative agreement with the bureau, the Council for International Exchange of Scholars helps administer the Fulbright Scholar Program for faculty and professionals in 155 countries in every region of the world and in a variety of disciplines.

Cyprus is located in the Mediterranean, east of Greece, south of Turkey, west of Syria, and north of Egypt. It is the third-largest island in the Mediterranean, and a member state of the European Union. Due to its strategic location, Cyprus has a rich history, one that dates back to the tenth century BC. Its position has made it an attractive target for military control and for economic trade. The Mycenaean Greeks,

Assyrians, Egyptians, Persians, Ptolemaics, Romans, Byzantines, French, Venetians, Ottomans, and British have all been interested in establishing control over the island.

While centuries of occupation brought a cultural legacy and cultural diversity to Cyprus, it also resulted in ethnic and religious conflict among the different Cypriot communities, as well as political disputes among the country's governing bodies. A month after the Republic of Cyprus became independent from the British in 1960, it joined the United Nations. The constitution of the Republic of Cyprus, which came into effect on the day of independence, was intended to balance the interests of both the Greek Cypriot and Turkish Cypriot communities. Cyprus, Greece, Turkey, and the United Kingdom entered into a treaty to guarantee the basic provisions of the Cyprus constitution and territorial integrity of Cyprus (UNFICYP, 2012).

Despite this treaty, the accumulated tension between the Greek and Turkish Cypriot communities resulted in the outbreak of violence in 1963. United Nations peacekeeping forces were deployed to Cyprus

Figure 4.1. Control Tower of the Nicosia International Airport. Photo by Constantia Constantinou.

in 1964 to prevent further fighting. In 1974, the conflict escalated into a war that divided Cyprus into two sections, north and south, and they have kept Greek and Turkish Cypriots separated to this day. The UN Security Council mandated that the peacekeeping force stay on the island, try to maintain a ceasefire, and guard the buffer zone that still divides the country.

I arrived in Cyprus in December 2005 as a Fulbright Senior Specialist. My assignment entailed working with librarians at the University of Cyprus in the southern Greek Cypriot sector. My objective was to develop a reference and user services department for the libraries.

The University of Cyprus was established in 1989 and admitted its first students in 1992. It was founded in response to the growing intellectual needs of the Cypriot people, and is well placed to fulfill numerous aspirations of the country. Admission for the majority of undergraduate students is by entrance examinations organized by the Ministry of Education and Culture. The first class consisted of 486 students. During 2010–2011, 4,691 undergraduate students attended courses offered by twenty-one departments, and there were 1,549 graduate students (University of Cyprus, 2012).

University of Cyprus Libraries employs approximately fifty professionals. Its collections contain 267,289 books, with an annual increase of approximately 12,000 titles. Some important collections include Cyprus studies, the archaeological collection, and Turkish studies. The library's mission is to serve the information and learning needs of the academic community (undergraduate and graduate students, academic staff, researchers, and administrative staff), while providing information services to the broader scientific community of the entire country (University of Cyprus Libraries, 2012).

Cyprus's library culture and practices, like those of many European countries, are quite different from those of American librarianship. The concepts of reference services, bibliographic instruction, and information literacy are not emphasized. Ideas such as the teaching mission of a library or library instruction are not familiar concepts. Cataloging, acquisition, information systems, and technical services receive more emphasis in personnel allocation and strategic planning efforts.

To create a reference unit, I had to first work with librarians and professional staff to evaluate concepts and principles of reference and user services. I organized a series of lectures, seminars, and workshops on topics, including pedagogy of reference services and research techniques, marketing and promoting reference services, information literacy, and assessment of reference services. I worked closely with librarians, teaching faculty and academic leadership to facilitate a curriculum design that incorporated the university libraries' resources. Since the concept of reference services presented the new idea of librarians as information specialists, and in some cases, subject specialists, it was important to cultivate a climate that fostered and promoted information literacy among faculty, librarians, and students.

Other projects included reviewing operational procedures, assisting with the library's strategic planning, participating in discussions to evaluate and assess a new library information system, as well as facilitating discussion among Cypriot academic and research libraries to establish the Cyprus Library Union Catalog. This work laid the foundation for strong professional associations, friendships, and building trust that would allow me to return to Cyprus six years later.

In 2011, I returned to Cyprus as a Fulbright Scholar. The objectives of my assignment were much broader, because they would have international implications. This project involved working with the two divided Cypriot communities. As mentioned, the Cypriot Turks and the Cypriot Greeks have been separated and isolated from each other since 1974.

In July 1974, Turkey, using as a pretext the coup against the legal government of the Republic of Cyprus, invaded the country in violation of the UN Charter and fundamental principles of international law. The consequences of this invasion and subsequent military action by Turkey are still felt today. The military occupation, forcible division, violation of human rights, massive colonization, cultural destruction, property usurpation, and ethnic segregation imposed since Turkey's military invasion remain the main characteristics of the status quo on the island (Permanent Mission of the Republic of Cyprus to the United Nations, 2012).

Today the two communities exist without any infrastructure permitting communication. There is no telephone system, cellphone satellite reception, or postal service to enable any type of communication or interaction between the North and the South. An individual crossing the United Nations-guarded borders, which is only allowed for a maximum of twelve hours, cannot communicate with the other part of Cyprus. In most areas of Turkish-occupied Cyprus, time stopped as of July 1974.

When I returned to Cyprus in January 2011, reform and social revolution were occurring in the Middle East, starting in Libya, Egypt, Yemen, and Syria. During the Arab Spring, the entire political climate was charged with demonstrations, street violence, and attempts to overthrow governments.

Six months before my arrival, the *New York Times* had published an article, "Letter from Cyprus in a Divided Land: Lessons in Living

FIGURE 4.2. Nicosia International Airport. Photo by Constantia Constantinou.

FIGURE 4.3. Cyprus Airways plane grounded on the runway since 1974. Photo by Constantia Constantinou.

Together," by Nick Thorpe (August 15, 2010). He interviewed a group of Jews, Muslims, Christians, and secularists from fifteen countries visiting Nicosia, Cyprus's divided capital. He asked Father Ngabirano, a Catholic priest from Uganda, what he would remember from his trip to Cyprus. The priest responded, "The challenge is to apply what I have learned here without being regarded as a traitor by my own community—or a spy by the other."

The events of Arab Spring and this *New York Times* article brought me to the hard realization that developing trust was to become the most crucial element of my work with Cyprus's Greek and Turkish communities. My status is unique. Though I am an American citizen, I am a native of Cyprus, being of Greek Cypriot descent. I had to be able to connect with, earn the trust of, and work closely with both communities as a true friend. Navigating the political and human conflicts cultivated in this troubled region for centuries would be the most significant and challenging aspect of my work.

I started by establishing positive relations with the Office of Public Affairs at the American Embassy in Nicosia. Through a series of meetings and consultation sessions, I was able to comprehend the different political dynamics encountered in the two communities. Even though I was a Cypriot national and was well informed about the cultural and political sensitivities of these two communities, my meetings proved invaluable for information sharing and reflection on daily events. The American Embassy's Office of Public Affairs introduced me to the local Fulbright Commission officers in the Greek and Turkish Cypriot communities. They became my liaisons to their respective university communities, as well as to other library communities, including public libraries, monastic and research libraries, and medical and special libraries.

The scope of my proposed project was twofold: (1) to work with the Greek Cypriot and Turkish Cypriot universities to address their individual library challenges and assist with their future planning and aspirations, and (2), to promote understanding while honoring cultural, ethnic, and religious differences.

I soon realized that language is not only the means of communication, it also facilitates deeper understanding of culture through humor, songs, and idioms. While I speak Greek fluently, I know very little Turkish. I resolved to improve my Turkish language skills by attending intensive evening classes.

I then turned my efforts toward the next level of international collaboration by completing an agreement between OCLC's European network leadership team and Cyprus. As a result, the largest university library in Cyprus was able to join the global bibliographic system, providing the foundation for a robust national library system.

It became imperative to find ways to promote understanding between the Greek and Turkish Cypriot library communities while honoring cultural, ethnic, and religious differences. The approach I adopted involved asking the Office of Public Affairs if I could develop library programs of seminars, lectures, and conferences that involved both communities. Through the support of the U.S. State Department, I was able to invite Cornell University Libraries director Anne Richardson Kenney to Cyprus to present on the topic of library collaboration. Her lecture on the Cornell-Columbia 2CUL cooperative consortial model demonstrated the type of possible collaborations among different institutions.

Through a highly politically and ethnically sensitive process, elected officials, librarians, and educators from these war-torn communities attended a one-day conference hosted at the Cyprus Fulbright Center, located in the neutral UN buffer zone. The conference gave librarians and educators a chance to meet each other for the first time, diminish their perceptions of each other as enemies, and explore ideas of mutual benefit, trust, collaboration, and cultural understanding.

The event was successful. I then collaborated with the State Department to write a grant sponsoring the visit of two Cypriot librarians (one

FIGURE 4.4. Greek Cypriot and Turkish Cypriot librarians gathered at the Nicosia Fulbright Center for the Anne R. Kenney Lecture on collaboration among libraries, April 2010. Photo by Constantia Constantinou.

Figure 4.5. Anne R. Kenney shaking hands with ex-Minister of Education, Cyprus (Dr. Sofianos) and Executive Director of Cyprus Fulbright Commission (Daniel Chajitofi) during a reception before the lecture, April 2010. Photo by Constantia Constantinou.

Figure 4.6. Greek Cypriot librarians host a luncheon for Turkish Cypriot librarians at chateau restaurant in Nicosia, Cyprus, at the United Nations Buffer Zone, April 2010. Photo by Constantia Constantinou.

Greek and one Turkish) to the United States. The purpose of this trip was to engage the librarians in a deeper understanding of the diverse but highly collaborative practices of American academic and research libraries. They were able to visit and discuss library practices with librarians at the State University of New York, Cornell, and Columbia.

I was still trying to make a real and lasting impression in the separate worlds of these two library communities. *Trust* is never a given—it is earned, and it is always put to the test, especially in communities where religious, racial, political, and ethnic conflict has been cultivated for centuries.

During the final days of my assignment, while visiting one of the major Turkish Cypriot libraries, a librarian showed me a book from their special collections. In that moment, the two divided worlds of Greek and Turkish Cypriots finally came together: the book was published in Istanbul in 1884 and written in the Greek alphabet. Since they knew I could read Greek, they asked whether I could explain the monograph's origin and content. According to a handwritten Greek inscription on the title page, the book belonged to a Greek woman who lived in Istanbul at the turn of the twentieth century. When I read the book, the words made no sense to me. But when I read it aloud to the Turkish librarians, their eyes lit up with an expression of understanding. They began to discuss the book in Turkish. I was still mystified, however, since the text in Greek had meant nothing to me. In fact, the Turkish Cypriot librarians understood my spoken words because the Greek text gave a phonetic pronunciation of Turkish words! This publication, phonetically pronouncing the Turkish text, was printed in the Greek alphabet. Immediately, we recognized the book as a rare type of printed work called a Karamanlidika, the language of the Karamanlides, used by Turkish-speaking Orthodox Christians of Cappadocia, a region of the troglodytic ecclesiastical and monastic communities of the Byzantine Empire.

At that moment, there was an incredible realization of how the lives of the Turks and Greeks have been deeply intertwined and their fates inseparable, even though they have remained divided throughout the centuries.

As my project neared completion, I started to spend more time traveling through the countryside in both sections to gain a better understanding of people through their daily lives. One warm day, while traveling to a monastery, I passed through a small village. There I came upon a sign

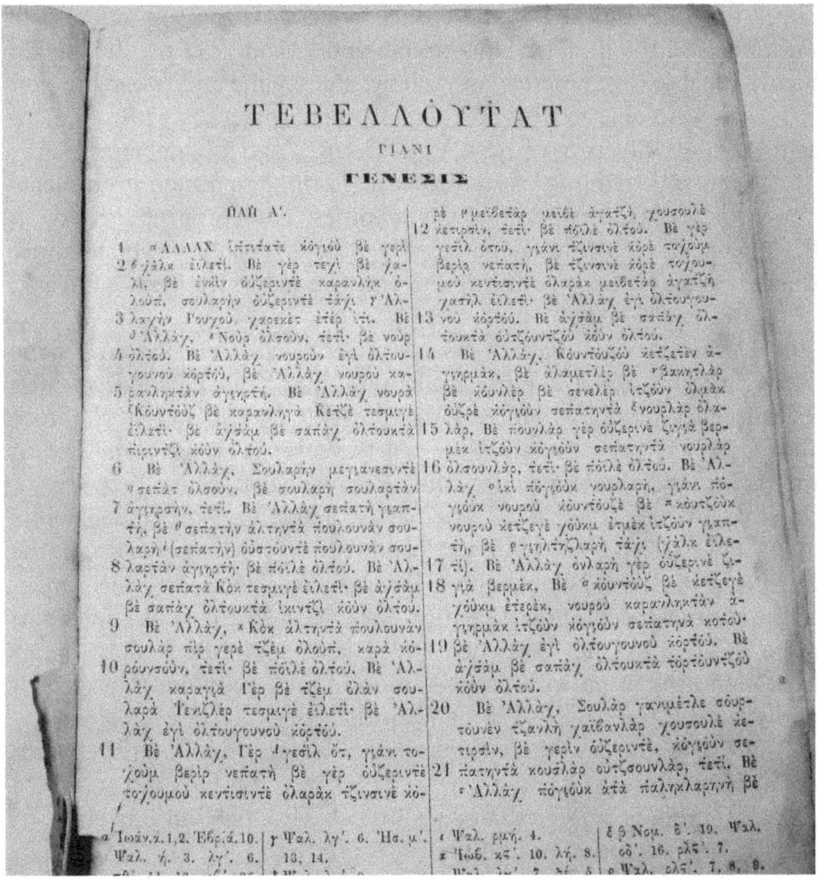

ΤΕΒΕΛΛΟΥΤΑΤ

ΓΙΑΝΙ

ΓΕΝΕΣΙΣ

ΠΑΪ Α'.

FIGURE 4.7A. Old Testament, Istanbul, 1884. Photos by Constantia Constantinou, March 2010.

in the middle of the main road. With Greek letters, the sign spelled the words *Bibliotheke* = *Demokratia* + *Kritike Skepse* (Library = Democracy + Critical Thinking). I drove back to the village and looked around to find the library, and perhaps the librarian who placed such a great sign in the middle of the road, but I couldn't find one. This small village is a farming community of 300. It has one grocery store, one school, three churches, but no library. Yet this sign conveys an important message that library scholars have tried to teach about in classrooms, conferences, and seminars throughout their entire careers. It all comes down to this message, discovered on a sign in the middle of the road, in a small village with no library: Library = Democracy + Critical Thinking.

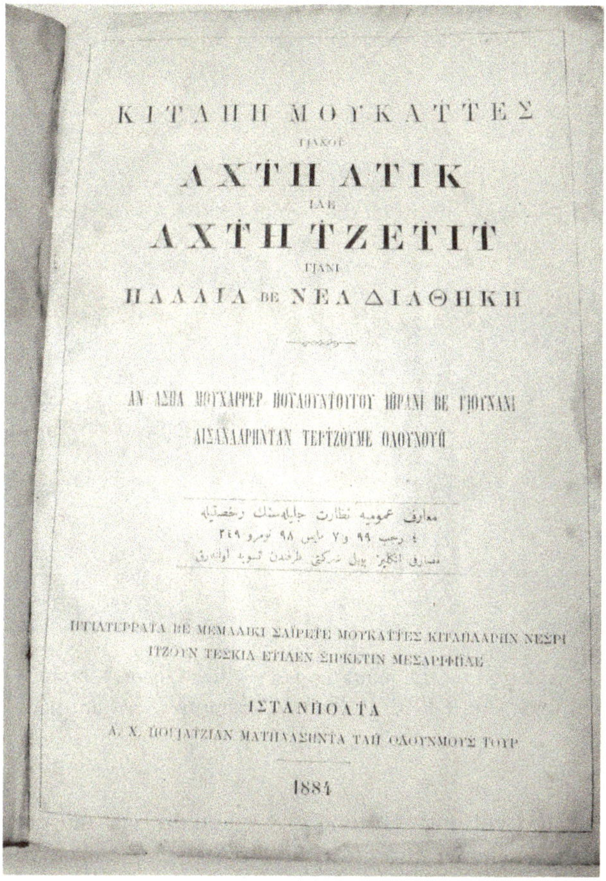
ΚΙΤΑΠΗ ΜΟΥΚΑΤΤΕΣ

ΑΧΤΗ ΑΤΙΚ

ΙΛΕ

ΑΧΤΗ ΤΖΕΤΙΤ

ΓΙΑΝΙ

ΠΑΛΑΙΑ ΒΕ ΝΕΑ ΔΙΑΘΗΚΗ

ΑΝ ΑΣΗΑ ΜΟΥΧΑΡΡΕΡ ΠΟΥΑΘΟΥΝΤΟΥΓΟΥ ΙΠΡΑΝΙ ΒΕ ΓΙΟΥΝΑΝΙ
ΛΙΣΑΝΛΑΡΗΝΤΑΝ ΤΕΡΤΖΟΥΜΕ ΟΛΟΥΝΟΥΠ

معارف عموميه نظارت جليله سنك رخصتيله
٤ رجب ٩٩ و ٧ مايس ٩٨ نومرو ٣٤٩

ΙΠΤΙΛΑΤΕΡΡΑΤΑ ΒΕ ΜΕΜΑΛΙΚΙ ΣΑΪΡΕΪΕ ΜΟΥΚΑΤΤΕΣ ΚΙΤΑΠΛΑΡΗΝ ΝΕΣΡΙ
ΙΤΖΟΥΝ ΤΕΣΚΙΛ ΕΤΙΛΕΝ ΣΙΡΚΕΤΙΝ ΜΕΣΑΡΙΦΙΛΕ

ΙΣΤΑΝΠΟΛΤΑ

Α. Χ. ΠΟΓΙΑΤΖΙΑΝ ΜΑΤΠΑΑΣΗΝΤΑ ΤΑΪ ΟΛΟΥΝΜΟΥΣ ΤΟΥΡ

1884

FIGURE 4.7B. New Testament, Istanbul, 1884. Photos by Constantia Constantinou, March 2010.

History, particularly in the Middle East, has repeatedly demonstrated that peace and coexistence are not inevitable. Trust, peace, friendship, and collaboration are not always achieved by treaties, governments, or political leaders. More often, peace, understanding, and conflict resolution are achieved through the extraordinary efforts of common people, such as the teachers, educators, and librarians I have come to know and respect through my work in Cyprus.

International library work requires specific refined skills. As scholars of our discipline, mentors of practice, and advocates for freedom of expression, we work with our international partners to strive for common understanding. We honor diversity and acknowledge and respect

FIGURE 4.8. Greek sign on the main road of a village reads: Library = Democracy + Critical Thinking, April 2010. Photo by Constantia Constantinou.

the political and cultural awareness of communities and countries. As guests in others' homes, libraries, and nations, we open ourselves to learn from our hosts. We discover that there are no universal solutions and no universal practices. Frequently, we discover that solutions are embedded in the roots of each community, each culture, and each ethnic identity. We do not impose ideas from our own preconceived methods and practices. Instead, we collaborate to uncover results, solutions, and ideas that derive from the host country and its citizens.

Senator J. William Fulbright, on the occasion of the thirtieth anniversary of the Fulbright program in 1976, stated:

> International educational exchange is the most significant current project designed to continue the process of humanizing mankind to the point, we would hope, that men can learn to live in peace—eventually even to cooperate in constructive activities rather than compete in a mindless contest of mutual destruction. . . . We must try to expand the boundar-

> ies of human wisdom, empathy and perception, and there is no way of doing that except through education. (Fulbright International Education Exchange Program, 2012)

Despite the challenges of the small and troubled country of Cyprus—a nation that remains divided by borders, barbed wire, sandbags, political conflict, and religious beliefs—there is always a spirit of enlightenment that rises above differences to reveal our humanity and unites us in a common purpose.

REFERENCES

Fulbright International Education Exchange Program. (2012). *Fulbright on International Exchange*. Retrieved from http://fulbright.state.gov/history/sen-fulbright/quotations.

Permanent Mission of the Republic of Cyprus to the United Nations. (2012). *Cyprus Problem in Brief*. Retrieved from http://www.cyprusun.org/?cat=74.

UNFICYP. (2012). *United Nations Peacekeeping Force in Cyprus*. Retrieved from http://www.un.org/en/peacekeeping/missions/unficyp/background.shtml.

University of Cyprus. (2012). Retrieved from http://www.ucy.ac.cy/goto/main-portal/en-US/BriefHistory.aspx.

University of Cyprus Libraries. (2012). Retrieved from http://library.ucy.ac.cy/ENGLISH/general_infoE/geninf_lib_en.htm.

THE UNFINISHED WORK

*Organizational Democracy**

John Lubans, Jr.

In spring 2015 I taught my fourth eight-week-long class, the Democratic Workplace, at the University of Latvia in Riga. Aimed at librarian practitioners and graduate students, the class introduces democratic concepts pertaining to how people (not just librarians) organize to pursue their cooperative mission.

This paper discusses how the class came into being, explains its goals, and briefly describes its content and methodology. The methodology may be of interest to anyone engaged in training initiatives, because my approach is more of a "flipped" pedagogy than the lecture-and-textbook variety. I rely heavily on students teaching themselves and their peers—I expect students to coach each other and to take responsibility for their learning.

BACKGROUND

The present eight-week class began to take shape shortly after I received a Fulbright (2011) to teach in the Department of Information and Library Studies at the University of Latvia. I was open to rethinking

*Abraham Lincoln at Gettysburg, November 19, 1863, spoke of the "unfinished work" (democracy); that it was up to the American people to confront this "great task," ensuring "that government of the people, by the people, for the people, shall not perish from the earth" (Lubans, September 18, 2013).

how and what I wanted to teach, and I had encouragement from the department head, Dr. Baiba Holma, to bring my own style to teaching the required Management of Information Organizations. The makeup of this first class—one-half graduate students and a mix of practitioners from the National Library of Latvia and University of Latvia libraries—set a pattern by which students could complete a graduate-level class and practitioners could earn a continuing education certificate.

Clearly, without support from the leaders of these two institutions (Director Andris Vilks of the National Library and Dr. Iveta Gudakovska of the University Libraries), this class would not have benefited from the positive mix of practitioners with students. Each group brought its unique perspective and experience to the class. And there was the potential benefit of exposing (and challenging) current and future practitioners to dramatically different ways of organizing the workplace. When preparing for the 2011 Fulbright, it dawned on me that instead of merely tweaking my usual management class to fit a foreign audience, I now could test the leadership concepts I'd been promoting for the last several years, which can be encapsulated in the phrases "leading from the middle" (Lubans, 2010), the "unboss" (Lubans, 2006), and the idea of a "post-departmental library" (Lubans, 2009).

I've broken away deliberately from the ubiquitous lecture-and-textbook teaching model (which is prevalent in both free and not-so-free societies). My emphasis is, instead, on working in teams, leading and following, with the students thinking independently and critically in class and in group discussion among peers in their native language, and on questioning authoritarian rule (with all its coercive certainties) versus democratic rule (with all its ambiguities). This emphasis is specific to creating leadership and workplace options in a posttotalitarian culture. That said, my approach to teaching these concepts could just as well be used—and indeed is used—in some American classrooms to the benefit of many students who are not permitted as much freedom as they may want in their learning.

A musical group's democracy also influenced the design of the Riga class. For years I've been studying the celebrated (and conductorless) Orpheus Chamber Orchestra. Orpheus partners with two music schools in New York—Juilliard and Manhattan—to train student orchestras to develop concert programs, rehearse, and perform, all without a conductor or boss (Lubans, 2006). Orpheus's professional musicians coach student orchestras to help them grasp and apply the Orpheus process, and to thoroughly understand what it means for a group of musicians to play without someone telling them what sound to make.

Much was and is learned via these experiences—when every musician's *inner conductor* manifests herself. The student musician realizes he has an opinion, and can offer a personal, valid interpretation of the music. The student musician, taking responsibility for the whole piece of music, hears the music differently. No longer does she hear only her section, now she listens to and hears (and supports) the whole orchestra. The holistic musician adjusts her playing to the music of the orchestra, not just to the score in front of her.

This influenced my class design. I especially tried to counter the tendency for a coach or professor to direct, to intervene like a conductor or micromanager when things were not going smoothly. A coach may need to intervene, but only after students have given it their all and perhaps made mistakes, but not before. I wanted my Riga students to develop skills of self-management and to correct themselves rather than leaving it to me to direct.

I already knew that, while students may want to work in groups, they don't necessarily have the skills to do this as well as they would like. Some of the very best students, indeed, view group work as futile because they wind up, martyr-like, doing most of the work for little credit. Old ways—being told what to do or "letting George do it"—die hard.

After my 2011 Fulbright semester, I applied for the Fulbright Senior Specialists Program, which I was awarded in 2014. As part of my application, I built the prototype of the eight-week Democratic Workplace. In early 2013, I taught the inaugural class, Democracy in the Workplace: Self-Managing Teams and Managing Self, for credit at the University of Latvia. It enrolled sixteen students, half master's degree students and half librarian practitioners, who met once a week for three hours. Latvia, a democratic nation since 1991 and a member of the European Union and NATO since 2004, has endured centuries of external rule and imposed government.

The class explored several concepts, including freedom at work, teams and teamwork, group dynamics, self-management, leadership, and effective followership. It was designed to offer alternative ideas to those inherited from the pre-1991 Communist era, as well as post-1991 examples of Western organizations, largely the hierarchical, top-down model. My intent was that by the end of the course students would have well-formed answers to these and other questions: What is (or is not) a democratic workplace? Can a workplace team be self-managing? How do teams develop and perform? What are the traits of democratic team leaders, and what do they do? How can democratic teams and concepts exist in a bureaucracy, in a hierarchy? What does "freedom at work" mean? Importantly, I wanted each student to better understand who he or she is as a leader and follower, including his or her preferred way of leading and following.

Through my students' work and discussion, I continue to develop understanding and definition of a democratic workplace. I keep learning that the effects of a long-term totalitarian culture have more than a single generational effect—attitudes and values developed during the pre-1991 Communist era linger and influence today's behaviors. This last statement could apply to all nations who have suffered under totalitarian rule. The question is, after metaphorically slaying the ogre and gaining independence, what do we want to be? We know what we do not want: despotism. But what do we want? What can any organization do to advance movement and avoid the stagnation that may descend after a joyous return to liberty?

RATIONALE

My own philosophy is that a team-based, democratic approach is the best way to achieve a flexible, proactive organization, responsive to change, with the highest productivity and outstanding service. I have seen this happen time and time again.

Yet I eschew any evangelization of democracy, and the idea that American organizational models are inherently superior. Hardly! We in the United States have much to learn from other models and cultures of organization and types of leadership. My purpose is not to convince that the democratic workplace is the only way; rather, it is to help students understand how a democratic workplace stands apart from the hierarchy.

I do try to demonstrate how and why libraries and other organizations that invite and encourage staff participation perform better—are more productive and innovative—than organizations that limit staff involvement. I provide a practical and realistic perspective on how democratic ideals can be applied to the workplace by drawing on my experience in leading change initiatives and directing self-managing teams.

THE CLASS

While flipped, the class still uses many traditional techniques: lectures on theory and practice; small-group guided discussion in Latvian of assigned readings, films, literature (including children's books), and case studies; a student-team project and presentation (see Example Assignment 1), solo papers (see Example Assignment 2); and an array of experiential activities, a low-risk, tested way for students to learn for themselves many democratic concepts.

If you have students who want to be challenged, who want fresh perspectives, who want to learn about themselves, and who want to work with other people to do a good job, then the best thing is to deemphasize the lecture and increase opportunities that help hone skills in working with others—leading, following, or both—and in understanding the dynamics of why some groups reach their goals and why others drift.

However, there is a downside to deemphasizing the traditional classroom. David Hestenes, one of the pioneers in the flipped classroom movement, says, "Students have to be active in developing their knowledge. They can't passively assimilate it" (Hanford, 2012). Alas, some students prefer the lecture model because it is less demanding than peer teaching. With the peer-teaching model, you have to do the assigned work before class; a lecture-only approach permits procrastination until the final memory exam. This traditional lecture model is prevalent, with colleagues posting their lectures online and not expecting students to physically attend class. That is why I make clear that a student must opt in to attend class and actively participate.

On the first day, students as a group must define what it means to participate and be a team member, not a soloist. Somewhat warily—and with the realization I am not going to tell them, and that much of their grade depends on participation—they begin to define what they want from their classmates, and to what they are willing to commit. These participation expectations are written and distributed, and revisited throughout the course as needed.

While few fully democratic organizations exist in the world of work, there is an observed tendency in organizations to flatten out, to work in teams, to collaborate. The increasing use of task forces in libraries that bring together department heads, line librarians, and support staff suggests that the *post-departmental library*—a far more democratic organization—is evolving (Lubans, 2009). The hierarchy remains in place, but many administrators have realized that some better decision-making is made outside the executive suite. Lately, I have begun to consider these melded organizations as hybrids (Lubans, February 4, 2014). Students entering the information profession now need to understand that the administrative landscape has changed, and that they might be expected to work in groups, across the library, not just in one department. They would be expected to work together: unit or departmental interests are now subordinate to the overall organization. They would be expected to be effective followers, people with their own ideas and the ability to express, promote, and adjust those ideas. Even the most traditional libraries, those that are leery of any self-organization concepts, make it clear that they value job candidates who define themselves as flexible, open to change, and team players.

CONCEPTS FOR TEACHING THE DEMOCRATIC ORGANIZATION

Key Concept 1: Democracy

On the first day of class, I ask students to draw a picture of a "democratic workplace." Each student explains—in Latvian or English—what he or she drew. Then we discuss my working definition:

Many leaders
Decentralized power
Open books (finances and personnel)
Planning involves everyone
Team-based, flat organization
Many effective (independent and critical thinking and action-taking) followers
Managers do "real work"
No formal performance appraisal
Workers help define individual perks, from parking to pay
A proactive organization

Throughout the class, we discuss how a different kind of leadership is required in the democratic workplace: the "unboss." Here are some characteristics and qualities of the unboss leader:

Represents the organization
Collaborates in decisions and actions
Works alongside
Waits for others to initiate
Tolerates mistakes
Defends staff
Shares praise; accepts blame
Appreciates urgency and takes the long view
Listens and hears; questions and offers well-considered advice

Takes the job seriously; self, less so
And, most mysteriously and paradoxically, is someone, about whom the people exclaim, when the task is done, "We did it ourselves!" (Lubans, April 15, 2014)

Key Concept 2: The Three "Whats" of Experiential Learning

I rely on experiential learning to explain and augment leadership, management, and teamwork concepts. I am among the very few management instructors in library schools to use experiential activities. Certainly, many use team projects, but I know of no one else who uses group activities, at least to the extent that I do.

I've culled and adapted my problem-solving initiatives from the many new games created within the experiential education movement dating from the 1960s: Egg Drop, Bibliofoon (now called Book Chain), Mirage, Pyramid, and Frenzied Fun and Facts. Each of these activities can be accomplished in thirty to forty minutes.

The value is in the debrief following each activity. We explore the three "Whats":

1. The "What?" (the activity and what happened)
2. "So, What?" (what I learned about myself and the group during the activity)
3. "Now, What?" (what I will use or apply personally from what I learned from the activity).

Because these types of teaching and learning experiences are new and fun, it's important to emphasize the learning, to allow students time to think, reflect, and discuss what has been learned for the workplace. Another reflective technique is to require an individual written report on the most important takeaways.

Key Concept 3: Mix the Class

Just like in the United States, I make a point of mixing participants in every small group activity, so students can get to know each other. While students work, I observe (and photograph) each group's dynamics: I see a group of "strangers" become a supportive team, I see a few students initially reluctant to take part—standing off to one side, or leaning away from those leaning in. I see students engaging other students, welcoming them to speak up. In sum, just about every element of group dynamics, "form, storm, norm, perform" (Tuckman, 1965) is present, especially the difficult storming phase.

Groups that *succeed* in an activity often express pleasure in the behavior of the group—about how they all worked together, how all ideas were respected, how and why a good idea survived, and how they dealt with conflict. I italicize "succeed" because some of the best takeaways come from group "failure." At least, mixing participants helps break the ice and eases social interaction for students, an essential part of teamwork projects. Of course, the best students can draw parallels from the activity to readings and class lectures and other group work.

Do these activities and the regular mixing of participants guarantee an understanding of group dynamics? Within limits, activities are superior to a lecture-only approach. However, if someone is closed to learning, it matters little what you do. From an organizational development perspective, any negative behavior demonstrated can be highly diagnostic and offer an opportunity to address the observed ineffectiveness.

Key Concept 4: Team Building

I am keenly aware that when we try to develop teamwork in the classroom, we get mixed results. Even when I stress that teams do not form easily, that teams may have conflict that has to be worked through (and that conflict in the classroom is a lot safer than conflict in the workplace), some groups follow the usual pattern, avoiding conflict while a few students take charge—just like some of those student orchestras coached by Orpheus.

I find myself talking extensively about what it means to move from a newly formed team to a highly effective team. Hardly an upward trajectory, initial enthusiasm and seeming camaraderie usually collapse with a precipitous drop in interest, a marked tendency to procrastinate and mistrust. Indeed, some teams linger in this pseudo-team slough of despond. Only the best teams emerge, work through difficulties, and achieve success, getting past competing, even within the team, to genuine collaboration. These teamwork insights are all good lessons to experience in an academic setting for transfer, later on, to the workplace.

Key Concept 5: Assessment. "Plus/Delta"

I make use of a quick assessment tool—the Plus/Delta. It is a rapid listing by participants of what worked well and what could have gone better. I introduce this technique at the end of the second day, and use it again on the final day. I have the students create a group Plus/Delta for the team project: What did you learn about your team and yourself? What worked? What could have been better? I ask them to give me a copy in English of each team's self-assessment.

Lately, I've added a personal, more introspective Plus/Delta, separate from the team Plus/Delta. I found the individual Plus/Delta valuable in helping the student diagnose just how she contributed and what she would do differently.

Here are some quotes from the Delta, the "What I would do differently side:"

> Worry less
> Listen more to my team members
> I would maybe choose another team, because a person needs to be able to work with different people and that is experience
> Speak up (more) in meetings
> Don't speak when it isn't necessary
> Don't rely always on improvisation
> I would tell more about what I am going to do (to my teammates before doing it)

Here are a few brief comments from the "What worked well?" Plus side:

> Emotional support
> Fun (spent good time together)
> We did it all within the prescribed time period
> Aim was clear
> Each does real work
> All on one wave[length]
> One for all, all for one
> Trust to each other

Example Assignment 1: Books2Eat Team Project

Teams of three or four students will plan, produce, and present a Books2Eat entry representing a Latvian children's book, folk tale, or folk song.

Besides creating the baked and decorated item, the team will select the title, describe the chosen book or folk song—with a full English description of the book or song and author—gather ideas, design the cake or cookie, test the ingredients, and prepare the product. They then present the entry for tasting at our class on Day 6.

Each Books2Eat entry must display one or more of these qualities:

Cleverness in overcoming adversity
Leadership by a least-likely follower
The Golden Rule applied
Collaboration, working with others to succeed
Speaking up when others are too afraid to say anything
Innovating
Using resources wisely

Example Assignment 2: Interview Paper

This is a required paper in English, approximately 750 words in length.

Choose one of these three topics:

> **Topic 1.** Interview someone who worked both under the Soviet way of management and in a post-Soviet organization. In other words, the interviewee would have worked in an organization prior to 1991, and then in one after 1991.
>
> **Topic 2.** Interview a participant about leadership and followership in the Dziesmu un deju svētki 2013 (national song and dance festival occurring every five years in Riga, bringing together tens of thousands of participants and spectators). Interview a leader, dancer, singer, organizer, or volunteer.
>
> **Topic 3.** Interview a Latvian woman leader about her style of leadership. How do Latvian female managers (in and out of libraries) lead, and how do their ways of working set them apart from other styles of leadership?

From feedback and observation, I keep stressing the teamwork aspect since it has immediate application in the Latvian workplace. Given the seeming trend toward a more democratic workplace, albeit a hybrid, I do not think teamwork—real teamwork, not what passes for teamwork in too many libraries—can be overemphasized. My hope is that sharing all this information with students facilitates their individual learning about how they lead and how they follow. When these students are given the opportunity to lead, they will remember this class and its leadership philosophy, and do their fair share of completing the—as yet—unfinished work.

REFERENCES

Hanford, E. (2012). Physicists seek to lose the lecture as teaching tool. *National Public Radio, 1*. Retrieved from http://www.npr.org/2012/01/01/144550920/physicists-seek-to-lose-the-lecture-as-teaching-tool?sc=emaf.

Lubans, J. (2006). The invisible leader: Lessons for leaders from the Orpheus Chamber Orchestra. *OD Practitioner: The Journal of the Organizational Development Network*, 38: 5–9. Retrieved from http://www.odnetwork.org/publications/practitioner/samples.php.

Lubans, J. (2009). Peer coaching for the new library. In J. Varlejs, & G. Walton (Eds.), *Strategies for regenerating the library and information profession*, pp. 126–136. Munich: K. G. Saur.

Lubans, J. (2010). *Leading from the middle and other contrarian essays on library leadership*. Santa Barbara, CA: ABC-CLIO/Libraries Unlimited.

Lubans, J. (2013). Democracy: The mustard on the hot dog. Retrieved from http://blog.lubans.org/index.php?itemid=1978.

Lubans, J. (2014). The "unboss" leader. Retrieved from http://blog.lubans.org/index.php?itemid=2319.

Lubans, J. (2014). The dog under your desk. Retrieved from http://blog.lubans.org/index.php?itemid=2199.

Tuckman, B. W. (1965). Developmental sequence in small groups. *Psychological Bulletin*, 63(6), 384–399.

LIBRARIANS BUILDING DIGITAL LEARNING OBJECTS SUPPORTING CULTURAL UNDERSTANDING

The Fulbright-Hays Seminar Abroad in Morocco and Tunisia

Michael J. Miller

By receiving a Fulbright-Hays Seminars Abroad grant, I was able to travel to the Maghreb region in northern Africa. After exploring religious diversity in the region during the Arab Spring, I applied experiences and documentation from this seminar to develop digital learning objects in order to complete a required curriculum project. This narrative describes how my first major experience with international librarianship enabled me to develop digital learning objects (hereafter called "the project") for cross-disciplinary use in college course work.

International and Foreign Language Education (IFLE) is an office of the U.S. Department of Education with responsibility for "strengthen[ing] the capability and performance of American education in foreign languages and in area and international studies" (U.S. Department of Education, "OPE About"). This office administers the Fulbright-Hays Seminars Abroad Program, which offers international cultural exchange professional development opportunities for high school and college teachers and administrators. Briefly, the Fulbright-Hays Seminars Abroad offer targeted and intensive professional development opportunities for secondary and postsecondary faculty to enrich educational expertise. They also require that a curriculum unit be developed after participation in the seminar.

The seminar, Religious Diversity in the Maghreb: Morocco and Tunisia, was listed as a professional development opportunity, as partially described in the original IFLE announcement:

> The Maghreb is North Africa's rim set between seas and desert. Its past and present illuminate the diversity of religious traditions in western Islam. Morocco and Tunisia provide insights into the roles that Judaism, Christianity, and Islam have played in a part of the world that is at the same time African, Mediterranean, Arab, and Berber. This seminar seeks to draw lessons focusing on religious tolerance among the faiths in shared environments.
>
> The major faith of the region, Islam, will be seen in both countries through the lens of its own diversity. In Morocco, participants travel through time to discover in Fez how Islam was implanted in the "far west" of the Islamic world. At the same time, the focus of the diversity of faith within Islam will be revealed through the exploration of the religious orders of North Africa, the *zaouias*, and their significance in contemporary Morocco.

The trajectory of my grant-related activity led from the grant application process, through orientation, into the seminar itself, to postseminar development of the project, and then onward toward educational and professional networking activities. It should be noted that the seminar I participated in was similar in nature to a study-abroad program that students might experience in college or even at the secondary educational level.

The project I proposed to IFLE was called *The Way Forward: A Digital Case Study of Religions in the Maghreb*. It was framed to be a digital resource that could be consulted as a learning object by students and faculty of various colleges delving into interfaith, interethnic, and interracial dialogues in the course of their teaching and learning activities. The resulting website is a librarian-generated digital learning object. The content is composed of a multimedia compilation of writings, "talking points" tools, drawings, resource lists, photos, and audiovisual files. It explores lessons teaching religious tolerance in Muslim society, and is a rich resource for further exploration of the intercultural aspects of religious diversity. More specifically, it explores diversity *within* Islam in an effort to shed light on important differences that non-Muslims should come to understand.

I approached this grant-funded professional development opportunity as a librarian who wanted to expand my subject discipline repertoire by gaining a basic knowledge of religion and diversity topics. Having a background in the social sciences and librarianship, I believed this professional growth could inform my collection development and service program leadership activities at the academic library where I worked. I also wanted to put my additional background and training in educational technology and instructional design to good purpose. I believed I could achieve this dual goal by developing meaningful educational tools that could be shared on campus and with others across the profession.

Here is an excerpt from the project plan I submitted:

> *The Way Forward: A Digital Case Study of Religions in the Maghreb* will be aligned with and augment the "Search for Common Ground" dialogue program, which is part of the "Bridging the Cultural Divide" initiative of the CERRU [Center for Ethnic, Religious, and Racial Understanding at Queens College, CUNY]. . . . It will be developed on a portable web-based platform employing open source social networking software.
>
> It will include explorations of the lessons learned in Morocco about the historical factors that have yielded a religious tolerance in that Muslim society. It will explore diversity *within* Islam in an effort to shed light upon important differences that outsiders need now desperately to understand. It will provide examples of how various faiths survive and thrive in the midst of a majority Muslim land.
>
> It will also present representations of the cultural landscape of both Morocco and Tunisia which will be afforded by the planned trips to educational and religious institutions throughout the course of the seminar; depictions of the explorations of mosques and fortresses of Tunisia will add stimulating visual and textual substance to this digital case study. A record of discussions that were transacted with the religious students and leaders in Rabat and Tunis will be a rich resource for exploring the intercultural aspects of religious diversity in the region.

Having met all program requirements and submitted a successful online application, I received official notification of my award the following spring, just five weeks before the June 2011 departure date. Further minor administrative tasks ensued, and a detailed preliminary schedule arrived, followed soon by a hefty reading assignment. The study group was to receive lectures from particular authors represented in the preparatory readings, including Kenneth Perkins on Tunisia (Perkins, 2004); the famous Fatima Mernissi, author of *Beyond the Veil* (Mernissi, 1987) and *Dreams of Trespass* (Mernissi, 1994); and *Patience and Power* by Susan S. Davis (Davis, 1983). A full bibliography of many resources studied or referenced during the seminar is included on the project website (Miller, 2012).

Planning for the seminar was pretty straightforward since I am a frequent international traveler. I obtained everything from climate-appropriate clothing to emergency contacts and learning supplies. I took extra effort to ensure I could record my experiences in preparation for developing the project. I used tablets for note-taking in lectures; pads for drawing pictures of people, places, and cultural objects; and a Blackberry phone with superb photo and movie capabilities to help with digital documentation. These combined well with local Internet access and social networking applications to generate ongoing reports of the group's progress during the seminar. Further, I took a waterproof folder to keep my written materials safe, and a mesh bag for carrying all my technology peripherals.

The seminar itself, being driven by the mission of the Fulbright program, was a complete package designed to develop participants' intercultural competencies. With an historical orientation we received from area experts, the two-week language immersion program, our home stays, and cultural presentations at the language school, we had a substantial introduction to the culture and history of the Maghreb. When I submitted my program evaluation to the organizers, I recommended French language preparation as an essential addition. Because this had not been included, I was limited in my interactions with local residents. I also suggested that language learning could be more targeted to travel and more closely aligned to seminar topics.

Grant applicants were informed that they should be prepared to put their expectations aside as they pursued this undertaking. It took me a bit of time to set aside the original program description and schedule we were given, and relax and open myself up to all the learning possibilities offered as the *real* program unfolded throughout the six weeks. One must be prepared to adjust to changes in the schedule as situations dictate. After I did this, I had a wonderful learning adventure!

As mentioned above, lectures were delivered by area academic experts, artists, writers, and political leaders. Most lectures were enriching. We took excursions into the old centers (medinas) of each of the larger cities, exploring souks and mosques whenever possible. We also visited churches and synagogues. Organizers of the seminar scheduled a few free periods. Although restricted in number (probably due to the unstable political and social environment driven by the Arab Spring), these moments allowed for my most memorable independent explorations. Getting lost in the medinas twice, seeing a protest crowd chased by police, being pursued by commercially predatory merchants, and gaining independence and success in the souks all painted vivid images in my mind.

One of the most challenging aspects of the seminar was my own home-stay. While the family was accommodating, supplying the requisite space and meals, the family dynamics were uneven. The father seemed to discourage my interaction with his children, interrupting a language-learning exchange between me and his daughter. He often shooed his wife and daughter into the kitchen, out of my presence. He also constantly watched violent television shows, which further limited interaction during my stay.

On the upside, the household mother arranged to celebrate my birthday in her sister's home, hosting one of the other seminar participants. They prepared the coveted Moroccan chicken (*dejaj*) and couscous tagine to honor me that evening. The experience was quite delightful.

FIGURE 6.1. Mosque in a Djerbian menzel (Credit: Michael J. Miller)

I developed good discipline with my educational study and reporting activities, including keeping a daily journal. One thing I wish I'd done in preparation was develop my own list of "must-see" experiences, sites, institutions, and people before embarking. Although the program itinerary was very robust, when we were given time for independent exploration, I was underprepared. Further, I would recommend adopting a journalist's mindset. Be respectful, but *do not be shy!* Be prepared to try to talk with strangers every chance you get: from the other participants, to the lecturers, to inhabitants of places you visit. These personal interactions became most pivotal. Regarding journaling: make sure to be descriptive and elaborate in the entries. I found some entries were just shallow reviews of daily activities. More descriptive responses could have enriched the record of my adventure.

The Maghreb seminar took us to Rabat and Sale, Fes, Casablanca, Marrakesh, and Amezray in the High Atlas Mountains in Morocco. In Tunisia, the group travelled from Tunis in the north, with the ruins of ancient Carthage and the port city Sidi Bou Said; south to El Djem and the nearby ancient Roman ruins of Volubilis; to Sousse, Munastir,

FIGURE 6.2. Seminar group in the Rabat medina (Credit: Michael J. Miller)

and Mahdia; to Sfax and the islands of Kerkennah; and then, via air, to the island of Djerba. During this part of the trip, we had a fantastic guide, Tunisian author and journalist Hatem Bourial, who provided great insights during our immediate, post-Arab Spring seminar.

Synthesis of my materials and implementation of the design were intense. My documentation strategies, interviewing techniques, digital design skills, and program curriculum project requirements were all important in developing the digital learning object. Extensive planning for documentation proved useful and rewarding for recording resources others cited throughout the seminar. I further resolved to expand my talents in drawing, ending up with sketches of speakers we enjoyed, as well as drawings of many artifacts we viewed in museums.

I documented lectures and sites by taking copious photos, and I used video to capture cultural performances we enjoyed. I picked up travel brochures, restaurant menus, guides from religious institutions, and materials provided by lecturers. I also purchased mementos to support local economies. Again, the project website hosts some of my media objects (Miller, 2012).

So, what do we do with all of this intellectual and experiential stuff we've collected? This question nagged me throughout the length of the seminar. My compatriots were primarily faculty from various disciplines, and most of them would be able to follow the normal curriculum project

FIGURE 6.3. Sketches, diploma, and journal from Fulbright-Hays seminar (Credit: Michael J. Miller)

template set out by IFLE. They would develop single sessions for a course they regularly taught, augmenting it with learning goals and appropriate assignments. As a librarian, I had no such vehicle to which to tether a curriculum project. After sweating and simmering in the hot African landscape, I eventually returned to my grant narrative. Creating a cross-disciplinary, multimedia web-based learning object was where I needed to go. As the only non-course-teaching participant in our group, I had to take a different approach.

After reviewing my notes, I analyzed the raw content I had collected. I was able to distill it down to three meaningful themes: Diversity within Islam, Interfaith Dialogues, and Cultural Diversity within the Maghreb.

FIGURE 6.4. Landing webpage of the project (Credit: Michael J. Miller) http://qcpages.qc.cuny.edu/~mmiller/MaghrebIndexB.htm

The resources initially provided to participants, plus drawings, photos, films, and lecture notes, have to a large extent been incorporated into the project. I developed an extensive bibliography listing books, videos, films, and websites either discussed or discovered in subsequent research. Synthesis of materials and implementation of the design was demanding, yet also a great way to review all the information gathered during the seminar. This process helped remind me of great experiences we all had shared.

I observed others in our group interact more fully with local residents. Various relationships can be established during a seminar: with the family of home-stays, fellow participants, seminar leaders, and experts you might wish to invite back to your own institution. It is good to carry and share your business card and obtain contact information from people you encounter. In the future, I will definitely engage more fully.

Project sustainability is another challenge with digital learning objects. The project is an active website and can be checked periodically for maintaining connectivity. It could be augmented with Web 2.0 news feeds of interest. More content could be added manually, if I choose to further my explorations. And finally, to make it more discoverable, it could be registered into the Creative Commons database. Of course, the files are portable, which became important as I relocated from my previous institution to a new one. Unfortunately, my new institution provides no clear means for hosting content. I will continue to explore options to keep this project alive and accessible for educational access.

Postseminar educational activities included a personal commitment to outreach in my professional communities about Fulbrights and the experience afforded by this grant award. To date, I have shared my digital case study with Queens College students and faculty, and across City University of New York. Admittedly, it was difficult coordinating with individual faculty and students groups. The challenge of marketing offline or third-party learning objects that can be integrated into various courses became apparent. This may be typical in contemporary academic environments, where independent projects are highly valued and faculty are primarily interested in publicizing their own efforts. For this reason, you must aggressively apply professional networking skills in the planning stages and follow up educational efforts and partnerships to secure engagements.

I started by volunteering to lead workshops to develop digital materials for use in the academic environment. As a new library director, I will encourage library faculty to design digital learning objects to bridge content to student experience. Further, I've offered to speak on campus about Fulbrights as a study-abroad opportunity for student and faculty professional development. This resulted in two faculty lectures at my previous institution.

Our travel group has held two reunions. We revel in our shared experiences, keep up with personal developments, and continue to discuss topics we explored together. Having registered as a Fulbright alumnus, I receive frequent communications related to Fulbright-sponsored professional development programs and the successes of other grantees.

Lastly, I teamed with two other library colleagues who have participated in Fulbright programs, so we may exchange our unique experiences and share with library professional communities the value and benefits of participating in these programs. We presented a short panel at the 2012 State University of New York library conference (*Constantinou, Miller, & Schlesinger, 2012)*, and offered a fuller presentation at the 2012 International Federation of Library Association's satellite conference (Miller, *2012)*. Finally, we resolved to collaborate on this publication.

REFERENCES

Constantinou, C., Miller, M. J., & Schlesinger, K. (2012). Transcending boundaries to increase cultural understanding between countries: Advancing global cultural understanding through innovative library practice: Three Fulbright experiences. SUNYLA Annual Conference. New York, NY.

Davis, S. S. (1983). Patience and power: Women's lives in a Moroccan village. Cambridge, MA: Schenkman.

Mernissi, F. (1987). Beyond the veil: Male-female dynamics in modern Muslim society. Bloomington: Indiana University Press.

Mernissi, F. (1994). Dreams of trespass: Tales of a harem girlhood. Reading, MA: Addison-Wesley.

Miller, M. J. (August 8, 2012). Getting the most out of a Fulbright award: Religious diversity in the Maghreb, Morocco and Tunisia. Transcending Boundaries to Increase Cultural Understanding Between Countries, a satellite conference for the 2012 World Library and Information Congress of the International Federation of Library Associations and Institutions. Lappeenranta, Finland.

Miller, M. J. (2012). Maghreb readings, media & other resources. Lessons from the Maghreb: Exploring a diverse Morocco and Tunisia. Retrieved from http://qcpages.qc.cuny.edu/~mmiller/Maghreb_Mats.htm.

Perkins, K. J. (2004). A history of modern Tunisia. New York: Cambridge University Press.

U.S. Department of Education, Office of Postsecondary Education—International and Foreign Language Education. (2014). Retrieved from http://www2.ed.gov/about/offices/list/ope/iegps/index.html.

CAPE CRUSADE

Building the Steve Biko Centre's Library and Archive in South Africa's Eastern Cape

Kenneth Schlesinger

During winter 2011, I travelled to South Africa as a Fulbright Senior Specialist for a six-week research project. The Fulbright Program offers short-term residencies to scholars in a variety of fields. Sponsored by the University of Fort Hare (Nelson Mandela's alma mater), I worked with the Steve Biko Foundation (http://www.sbf.org.za/home/) in both the Eastern Cape and Johannesburg.

Steve Biko (1946–1977) was a South African student leader active in the liberation movement of the 1970s. He is known for developing the concept of "Black Consciousness" and fostering community empowerment for social change. Unfortunately, Biko was brutally murdered by the police while in detention. However, his tragic death focused worldwide attention on the struggle against apartheid. The Steve Biko Foundation, headed by his son Nkosinathi, is dedicated to celebrating his legacy and political consciousness through programs of education, community activism, and youth empowerment.

The Foundation ambitiously resolved to construct the Steve Biko Centre, a cultural heritage institution based in Biko's hometown, Ginsberg Township (part of King William's Town on the Eastern Cape). Purposely situated in the heart of the township, its mission is to support community education, employment training, and economic development. Consisting of a museum, auditorium, conference center, commu-

FIGURE 7.1. Steve Biko exhibition. ©2011. Kenneth Schlesinger. Used with permission.

nity garden, Internet café, multimedia lab, and library and archive, it is designed to be not a memorial but rather a locus for civic engagement, public dialogue, and activism. At the time I was brought on board, the library and archive still had no content plan, but Foundation staff definitely wanted it to interact and "talk to" the other component spaces.

My task was to design a three-year strategic plan for the library and archive. What had appealed to the Steve Biko Foundation in my selection was not only my background in libraries and archives, but my performing arts experience. They sought an individual who viewed libraries in the larger context of cultural assets. Apparently, I was their guy!

Fortuitously, I had visited South Africa the previous year for ten days as part of a visiting delegation of archivists through People to People International. Through this incredibly rich and intensive experience, we toured major archives and research collections in the country, and facilitated conversations on the nature of contested collections, repatriated archives, and related issues of preserving cultural heritage. Truthfully, I would never have been able to accomplish this Biko Centre project if I hadn't already had a strong network of South African archival contacts. For further preparation, I reviewed Verne Harris's *Archives and Justice: A South African Perspective*, as well as consulted with international archival specialists and South African scholars at U.S. universities.

As with an architect conceptualizing a new space, my first assignment was to have conversations with all the major stakeholders of the Centre. The Biko Foundation administration conducted two days of orientation to give me a big-picture overview of their mission and programs, their process of evaluating other international cultural centers, and their ideas and priorities for the library and archive. In my project plan, the first step was to undertake a needs assessment of the local library and education community.

Public library leaders were generous and eager to meet with me. I visited the small local King William's Town Library. It had limited and dated print resources and only one Internet terminal, for use by the librarian. However, it contained a large, heavily-used student lounge containing textbooks and curriculum support materials. East London Central Library, located in the large city near King William's Town, had a medium-sized collection, as well as special collections and resources for people with disabilities.

FIGURE 7.2. King William's Town Public Library. ©2011. Kenneth Schlesinger. Used with permission.

Further, the Foundation arranged meetings with local representatives from Eastern Cape provincial libraries, archives, and curriculum administration. Historically home to both the black intellectual and liberation movements, the Eastern Cape is South Africa's poorest province. Nationwide unemployment is 28 percent, and the student pass rate of 52 percent on matriculation exams (high school graduation) is the second-lowest in the country (Central Intelligence Agency, 2011). Not surprisingly, public school students are greatly underserved by libraries—in many cases, one library must serve ten schools. Notably, the majority of residents in the primarily rural Eastern Cape don't have access to libraries.

Because there was initial suspicion and distrust of my status as a visiting outsider, these administrative meetings were politically charged. I had to quickly observe and assimilate the business protocols of South Africa. As a consequence, I learned to begin meetings by introducing myself, discussing my background and qualifications, and then outlining my project in the most respectful, inclusive, and transparent way that I could.

These strategies, in part, served me well when I scheduled appointments to visit special collections at major university archives. Whereas my previous Fulbright experience in Vietnam encouraged me to declare I was visiting as a representative of the U.S. State Department, there was no receptivity to this in South Africa. On the contrary, there exists considerable suspicion of the U.S. government—and of government in general.

Since the mandate in American archives is to provide access to and share documents, I was admittedly shocked when in several significant instances archivists did not show me original documents related to Steve Biko or liberation movements. After our initial interview, I was directed instead to the public access catalog (which I could obtain online) or printed finding aids. Several archivists questioned the need for the Biko Centre to build its own archive, and even stated that it was in *competition* with their mission.

On the positive side, some supplied contacts to colleagues at related research collections. Another primary exception was the South Africa National Library, whose previous curator had illegally collected an impressive array of anti-apartheid materials, which were banned at the time. Another leading university collection referred me to an individual who had conducted interviews about Biko with prominent colleagues for a biography she had written. She agreed to work cooperatively with the Foundation to make copies of the audiotapes and transcripts available

FIGURE 7.3. South Africa National Library, Cape Town. ©2012. Kenneth Schlesinger. Used with permission.

once she secured releases from subjects. Lastly, colleagues at Mayibuye Archives at the University of Western Cape, home of the Robben Island Archive and probably the most extensive collection of liberation materials in the country, not only provided copies of voluminous finding aids, but agreed to share pertinent records by preparing a proposed Memorandum of Understanding with the Biko Foundation.

Equally critical to the preparation of this strategic plan were visits to major cultural heritage museums in Cape Town, Johannesburg, Port Elizabeth, and Pretoria. South Africa is blessed with some of the world's most outstanding museums. To contextualize the proposed library and archive within the country's cultural history, it was significant to evaluate how museums interpreted their narratives visually, and how successfully they connected to visitors and their local communities. Too numerous to mention and chronicle would be my inspiring sojourns to, among others, the Apartheid Museum (likened to the U.S. Holocaust Memorial Museum), Robben Island (where Mandela was imprisoned), Constitution Hill (site of a notorious prison, now home to the Supreme

FIGURE 7.4. Mayibuye Archive. ©2010. Kenneth Schlesinger. Used with permission.

FIGURE 7.5. Apartheid Museum. ©2010. Kenneth Schlesinger. Used with permission.

FIGURE 7.6. Robben Island. ©2010. Kenneth Schlesinger. Used with permission.

Court), Hector Pieterson Museum (named after a thirteen-year-old killed in the 1976 Soweto student uprising), the Slave Museum, the Bo-Kaap Museum (Muslim immigration), and the Voortrekker Monument (Afrikaner heritage).

After three weeks, I was invited to the Foundation's Johannesburg office to present my preliminary findings to the Content Team for the Centre. I introduced them to the library and archive's mission statement:

> The Steve Biko Centre Library supports the information and learning needs of the Eastern Cape community and visitors. It provides both print and online cultural heritage materials related to South African history and civilization, Black Consciousness, and the African diaspora.
>
> Functioning as a teaching library, it fosters research support, independent learning and student success through public and outreach programs. Further, it is committed to partnering with and supporting the information needs of the other programs affiliated with the Steve Biko Centre.
>
> The Archive serves as an onsite and remote resource collecting materials documenting the life, writings, political

> engagement, and community development philosophy of Steve Biko. Materials are made available to local and international scholars to support publications, exhibitions, and special projects. The Archive also partners with local schools to introduce students to primary source documents to enhance the curriculum. (Schlesinger, 2011)

It is critical that the library serves the entire Ginsberg Township community—from children in crèches (nursery schools) to pensioners (elderly). Print materials not only have to represent the range of reading levels, but also the breadth of African culture and civilization. The library will collect materials in languages reflecting South Africa and the Eastern Cape, primarily Afrikaans, English, Xhosa, and Zulu. Literacy reinforcement is the foremost priority, followed by the need to promote student success in preparing for matriculation exams. The library should also collect textbook and curricular materials. A related component is to compile a repository of school lesson plans and curriculum development documents to promulgate best practices for teachers.

Since South Africa experiences pronounced digital divide issues, patrons should be welcomed into the library by ten public access Internet terminals and an opportunity to print documents. Study tables in the central portion of the space encourage student group work, surrounded by circulating-book stacks. The back area contains comfortable reading chairs, magazines for browsing, display cases for literary or archival exhibits, and open space for lectures, readings, and children's groups (the Biko Foundation recently informed me that they will now construct a separate children's room). Adjacent to this area are the periodicals stacks and a secure archive reading room.

The project plan also contains an appendix of policies for establishing access and circulation, cataloging software, collection scope, donor and scholar agreements, and similar matters. The intention is to keep annual membership fees and/or book fines low to encourage widespread use.

The archive provides a more specialized facility for researchers and scholars, documenting Steve Biko's brief life, professional contributions, and political philosophy. In addition to formulating cooperative exchange agreements with related repositories, new collections will be actively solicited. Processing interns could be recruited from University of Western Cape's Museum and Heritage Studies diploma program. Further, a local history archive of Ginsberg Township will be constructed by community members contributing visual materials, artifacts, and documents.

This physical space will be supplemented by outreach, active programming, and professional training programs. The library should exist as its own cultural center with readings, lectures, and writing workshops conducted by local authors. The Centre's accompanying computer and multimedia labs can be annexed to facilitate information literacy training, Internet instruction, and classes in website design and Photoshop. Community youth can be trained in multimedia technology equipment to record oral history interviews with community elders as an additional archival resource. A proposed bookmobile will travel to outlying rural areas to distribute print books and offer limited access to computer technologies.

Admittedly, the Biko Centre's Content Team had preconceived and fairly traditional notions about how the library could function. Initially, they were surprised by the plan's emphasis on literacy, software training, and cultural enrichment, particularly how the library and archive were conceived to work in tandem with the computer and multimedia labs. One member, smiling, said, "It's not quite what we had in mind, but I think it will work." Then I showed them the budget, which they believed was achievable with additional fundraising.

Before traveling to South Africa, a few leading archival specialists cautioned me about the nature of international archival work, primarily on the financial sustainability and ongoing support for implementation of plans once the residency is completed. I was also advised on the limitations of being an outsider and the necessity to quickly grasp the complexities and behavior mores of a different culture. Even if one is intellectually prepared, there's no comparison to actually being there on the ground.

From my previous experience, I had learned of South African archives' uneasy relationship with their U.S. counterparts—joint digitization agreements where American universities somehow expected to assume ownership of the attendant cultural property. One South African librarian characterized this as *digital imperialism*, as we heard many stories of the *contested* nature of the nation's cultural assets, notably sensitive materials from the apartheid era.

On the whole, I cherished this unique opportunity to spend six weeks in a fascinating and stunningly beautiful country with a complex and embattled history. I was proud of my submitted plan—however skeletal—which I believed did justice to honoring Steve Biko's admirable principles of social justice and community leadership. My South African hosts and the majority of colleagues I encountered were warm, receptive, and supportive.

At the same time, international assignments always contain a fair share of frustration, setbacks, disorientation, and loneliness. Ultimately, it was precisely this dislocation that I welcomed because it fundamentally challenged my overarching intellectual concepts, social constructs, and basic cultural biases. It wasn't always easy: sometimes it was shoved in my face, but it ultimately proved rewarding for my personal development, professional contributions, and intimate understanding of my role as a citizen on this planet.

In June 2012, I had the opportunity to escort a group of Lehman College students on a ten-day community-service trip to South Africa. Through my network of contacts, I was able to design an intensive visit that combined sightseeing, service learning, and enrichment in cultural heritage about the apartheid era. One of the high points—there were so many!—was having our students meet renowned South African musician Hugh Masekela backstage after one of his wonderful concerts. Students—many of whom had never been outside New York City, let alone the United States—volunteered at Nkosi's Haven, a residential community for children and their families with AIDS and HIV.

I made arrangements for them to volunteer at Mayibuye Archives, where they processed anti-apartheid posters and T-shirts, as well as documentation of sports activities by the prisoners on Robben Island. When we visited this prison the following day, these materials contextualized and deepened their appreciation of South African history. At the historically black University of Western Cape, they met students who shared their experiences of growing up in postapartheid South Africa. The value of archival materials is that they can be shared, and bring history to life for the next generation.

REFERENCES

Central Intelligence Agency. (2011). *The world factbook*. Retrieved from https://www.cia.gov/library/publications/the-world-factbook/geos/sf.html.

Schlesinger, K. (2011). *Steve Biko Centre: Strategic plan for library and archives*. Unpublished manuscript.

RECOMMENDED READING

Callinicos, L., & Odendaal, A. (1996). Report on archives in South Africa. S. A. *Archives Journal*, 38, 33.

Harris, V. (2007). Archives and justice: A South African perspective. Chicago: Society of American Archivists.

Harris, V. (2001/2002). Nascence, renaissance, and the archive in South Africa. *S. A. Archives Journal*, *42*, 1.

Rodrigues, T. (2010). Preservation and access to public records and archives in South Africa. *Mousaion*, *28*(2), 164–165.

INFORMATION LITERACY AND ACCESS

TOGETHER WE ARE BETTER

International Collaboration Supporting Information Access in the Dominican Republic

Loida García-Febo and Adriana McCleer

In 2012, citizens and representatives from academic, private, and not-for-profit sectors from the United States and Dominican Republic united to establish an international collaboration to improve access to information in the Dominican Republic. The originating idea for this partnership was cultivated by five advocates, scholars, and practitioners in the areas of education, technology, health, and library and information science. They collectively understood the transnational social and political environment and the cultural and linguistic competencies that were key to fostering relationships with additional participants.

BACKGROUND

The Dominican Republic is the Caribbean nation that shares an island with Haiti. It is located west of Puerto Rico. The national population is approximately 10,257,724 (United Nations, 2015). Most Dominican households do not have Internet access (Oficina Nacional de Estadística, 2015). Dominican communities have a range of libraries: school libraries, public libraries, and academic libraries, all of which focus on serving students of various ages. A national library census reported numerous barriers to information access in Dominican libraries, including poor facilities, outdated collections, limited training for library staff, and lack of information literacy education (Polanco-Almonte and Álvarez Armenteros, 2012). Despite such barriers, internal initiatives exist to improve information access in the Dominican Republic, including the library census, which was conducted with the intention of transforming libraries to better facilitate social and economic development in the country. Additionally, since 1998 presidential initiatives have established eighty-seven Community Technology Centers in rural areas to provide digital information access, digital literacy education, and additional workshops. The work of Vice President Margarita Cedeño de Fernández in developing the Community Technology Centers received recognition and funding from the Bill and Melinda Gates Foundation via the 2012 Access to Learning Award to support development of additional sites.

Between 2005 and 2013, two U.S.-based philanthropic organizations, Educere et Curare Foundation and Seibo al Progreso Organization Wisconsin Inc., developed a number of health and educational initiatives throughout the Dominican Republic. This laid the groundwork for the organization founders to initiate information-access projects in their communities of origin. Dr. Manuel Thomas, from Santiago Rodriguez, is president and founder of Educere et Curare (2013), which focuses on improving the quality of education and health through research and study of the educational process at the local level. Efforts include implementing the latest technological advances in the classroom.

Marcos Hernández Goico, from San Pedro de Macorís, located in the east of Dominican Republic, is president of Seibo al Progreso (2013). Its mission is to generate conditions for human development through formation of values that support improving the well-being of members of society and helping individuals achieve an overall integral development. Having close personal and professional links to the Dominican Republic, the organization presidents were aware of pressing community concerns in various regions. They reached out to their Dominican contacts to secure on-site support, and to their U.S. contacts for collaboration to address resident concerns in their native country.

In 2009, two education scholars from University of Wisconsin–Milwaukee, Antrop-González and Dr. Simone Conceição, participated in a conference, Estado de la Educación en el Mundo: Perspectivas Globales para Realidades Locales (State of Education in the World: Global Perspectives to Local Realities). This conference, attended by 200 teachers, was organized to investigate local education conditions in the Dominican Republic, addressing curriculum development strategies to improve the quality of education. This allowed discussion facilitators and partners to build rapport with educational administrators and teachers around the country. The conference and subsequent collaborations laid the foundation for future joint projects.

ACCESS TO INFORMATION AND THE POWER TO CAUSE CHANGE

In 2012–2013, Educere et Curare and Seibo al Progreso sought to extend their projects. In discussion with Antrop-González, they learned about the School of Information Studies at University of Wisconsin–Milwaukee, as well as the information access studies of doctoral student and librarian Adriana McCleer. She was professionally connected to international librarian Loida García-Febo, president of Information New Wave, a nonprofit seeking to enhance education of diverse ethnic groups in the U.S. and developing countries. García-Febo contributed her expertise in global information access. They conducted ongoing communication to conceive projects that supported the development of information access in the Dominican Republic. These planning activities resulted in the organization of an educational conference at no cost to participants, held in February 2013 at Universidad Autónoma de Santo Domingo in Santiago. Community media outlets were eager to promote this conference and supported a live press conference, a video-recorded roundtable discussion about education and information access in the Dominican Republic, a televised moderated interview, and a live television program interview.

Approximately 450 faculty and students from the School of Education at two universities and teachers and librarians from across the country attended this Spanish-language gathering focused on education and opportunities to support information access in the Dominican Republic. Skills development and continuing education have proven to be vital for the progress of initiatives to provide access to information in a developing country in Latin America (Cramer & Boyd, 2013).

García-Febo was the featured speaker. Due to great demand for information about emerging technologies, she taught a full-day, free, interactive workshop in Spanish entitled Acceso a la Información y el Poder de Causar Cambios (Access to Information and the Power to Cause Change), divided into several sections. The first keynote centered on access to information as a tool for education, civic engagement, and empowerment. García-Febo shared examples of libraries, telecenters, Internet cafés, and community centers in developing countries providing access to information and affecting the development, health, and socioeconomic aspects of their communities. She also discussed adapting social media and online resources, particularly how libraries, students, and researchers can effectively utilize such tools for knowledge creation, dissemination, and collaboration. Online tools enabling collaborative work, teleconferences, document sharing, and event planning were introduced. Examples of emerging platforms used for education and collaboration were promoted, including online distance-learning resources, virtual learning platforms, and information and communication technologies. In addition to recommendations regarding the tools discussed, García-Febo presented strategies for developing policy and measuring impact.

Antrop-González offered a comparative overview of curricula used in the United States and Latin America. He presented distinctions among various educational curriculum models, including factory models and liberatory models, and discussed education's impact on shaping society. McCleer shared details of the subsequent "Alternative Spring Break" program as an opportunity for shared learning and knowledge building in Santiago Rodriguez, whereby information access in schools would be

FIGURE 8.1. Collaborative partners (left to right): Dr. René Antrop-González, Loida García-Febo, Dr. Genaro Rodríguez, Adriana McCleer, Dr. Manuel Thomas (Credit: Loida García-Febo)

addressed by Dominican and U.S. students and community members. She and Thomas discussed opportunities for growth, collaboration, and professional and scholarly exchange among various partner groups to continue this conversation about information access and education.

An important element of the conference was participant interaction, as the partners recognized the participants as key contributors. Throughout the day, they were encouraged to share their experiences and ask questions. Information resources were shared with citizens and staff working in libraries, schools, community centers, and other community access points. This collaboration promoted understanding of how access to information can provide resources to improve health, social, and economic conditions. The partnership sought to overcome barriers to information access that occur as a result of limited knowledge of information resources and technologies, as well as barriers to the technological infrastructure needed to meet basic and higher-level needs (Clark & Gomez, 2011).

ASSET-BASED COMMUNITY PARTNERSHIPS

The foundational characteristic of this collaboration was the Asset-Based Community Development model, which is asset-based, internally focused, and relationship-driven (McKnight & Kretzmann, 1993; Green, Moore, & O'Brien, 2006). Its fundamental philosophy is that the broader community must be engaged, and everyone has something to contribute. A similar approach has been successfully followed by READ Nepal in developing countries in Asia (Neuman, Khan, & Dondolo, 2008). Partners viewed the Dominican community as rich, acknowledging its wealth of culture, talent, and skills. They avoided becoming paralyzed by perceived deficiencies, problems, and needs. This did not mitigate the need for funding and additional resources, but "identif[ied], support[ed], and mobiliz[ed] existing community resources and capacities for the purpose of creating and achieving a shared vision." (Sharpe, Greaney, Lee, & Royce, 2000).

This asset-based approach follows a distinct path to creating change (Greene, 2009). The partners did not try to solve problems or prescribe solutions. Instead, they focused on assets, identifying available individuals and resources, then mapping these assets for starting points of action. Connections and collaborations were posited to facilitate active participation and contributions.

Community empowerment is critical for sustainability, as people will invest more in what they have worked to create. The asset-based approach views *people* as the solution to community issues (Greene, 2009). The partners with direct connections to Dominican communities invited friends and colleagues to get involved with planning and preparation, which empowered them to become partners, decision makers, and leaders. For example, the previous relationship between Thomas and the president of Asociación Dominicana de Profesores helped secure transportation for teachers around the country to attend the conference.

It is both challenging and rewarding to coordinate collaboration between various stakeholders within and outside communities and institutions. The concept and value of time was one major cultural distinction encountered in this international collaboration. There were varied opinions on publicity timelines, length of the program, and real-time event schedules. Collective negotiation of timelines and schedules necessitated a calm approach, sensitivity, and flexibility.

The conference highlighted a range of online information resources and provided instruction on maximizing their functions. Participants were interested in incorporating these resources into their personal and professional lives. However, technological infrastructure in schools, communities, and the country in general proved to be a challenge. Many resources required Internet access, and at times, high-speed Internet access. Finally, conference facilitators strove to avoid being exclusive experts regarding the educational and informational challenges that arose during discussions. They redirected questions to the larger group or back to the inquirer, so they could explore their own responses.

The most significant success was establishing an international network of individuals, organizations, and institutions interested in improving information access through education in the Dominican Republic. This network was enhanced by involvement of additional partners, such as schools and local media, who helped raise awareness through their regional and national reach. They are motivated to keep working on efforts to eliminate information access barriers, as expressed in conversations with partners in follow-up trips and emails.

Dominican and U.S. librarians discussed library processes and services, comparing and contrasting trends in print materials' storage and lending, as well as technological and policy issues. Librarians' capacity to improve information access is increased by collaboration, which can improve education, health, and economic development.

Sharing the results of this collaboration functions as a cascade, because it impacts lives locally, regionally, and globally. Best practices from this project have been distributed to the library community through dissemination of project outcomes in conferences, seminars, and publi-

FIGURE 8.2. International librarians (left to right): Adriana McCleer; Dario Genao, Director of UASD Library, Santiago Campus; Loida García-Febo (Credit: Loida García-Febo)

cations. By establishing carefully planned, researched, and documented models, partners provide information that helps others replicate and enhance the project.

Fostering relationships with partners and project participants was instrumental for the success of this project. All four professionals were of Latino background, from Dominican Republic, Mexico, and Puerto Rico, with distinct cultures and speaking different Spanish idioms. Partners needed to understand the skills needed to communicate with multicultural and multilingual populations. According to Satgoor and Schnuer (2005), awareness of cultural norms and sociopolitical understanding are needed to succeed in projects and partnerships that involve organizations from different countries. Partners had to analyze the local educational system, the history of the country, and regional differences, including the transnational social and political environment. They became familiar with the local culture, discussing language competencies and limitations and expressing interest in such matters as local food, music, and architecture. They patiently worked with participants to effectively discuss ideas, explain concepts, and teach. These cultural competences are highlighted by Mi (2005) for librarians working with multicultural populations. The team was careful not to judge, avoided bias and stereotypes, and practiced empathy in local environments, as recommended by Allard, Mehra, and Quayyum in their Intercultural Toolkit for Librarians (2007).

It was crucial to be aware of the importance in acquiring intercultural skills, identifying factors to enhance cooperation, and exploring how to overcome barriers. Further, according to Satgoor and Schnuer's (2005) recommendations for international work, these partnerships were based on mutual respect, the ability to compromise, flexibility, a clear understanding of roles, a shared vision, and ongoing communication. Compromises were made to select venues, schedule dates, develop an agenda, and prioritize topics to meet the needs of the community. Everyone demonstrated flexibility to modify meeting times to accommodate many conversations with local educators and visits to local media. Overall, partners were committed to frequent and clear communication about the ultimate goal of the project.

COLLABORATIVE OUTCOMES

Ongoing communication with participants and local partners, as well as comments received at the conference, presented evidence on the impact of this collaboration. During the conference, numerous participants approached the speakers to express their gratitude for bringing the workshop to their country. They expressed interest in sharing the content of García-Febo's presentation with classmates, family, and friends. They shared comments, reflections, and photos in real time using social media platforms. Online posts included messages such as, "Aprendí muchísimo [I learned a lot]," "Me sentí muy identificado con todo [I connected with everything]," "La información puede salvar vidas [Information can save lives]," and echoed information shared in the presentations.

In addition to using social media for personal purposes, participants expressed interest in using such tools for research and scholarship. The partners received messages via social media websites requesting more information on pursuing graduate studies and the benefits of using online networks for expanding their education. Students wanted to discuss their current academic situation, professional plans, and aspirations to study overseas.

Continued virtual communication with the Dominican university encompasses discussion of the educational and professional development interests of library staff. Participants were concerned about barriers to information access in their country due to lack of infrastructure and sought improvements. For instance, university library staff described the negative impact of outdated technology and low bandwidth on their services and users. They sought to develop collaborations and collectively address such issues.

Many participants were members of Asociación Dominicana de Profesores, which gave them the opportunity to discuss issues facing teachers nationwide. Antrop-González stated, "I felt much political will from many to make serious changes from the bottom up" (R. Antrop-Gonzalez, personal communication, May 30, 2013). Participants were energized personally and professionally by the presentations, the formal and informal discussions, and the opportunity to network with others. An assessment is under way to identify next steps, as professors and librarians have expressed a desire to continue relationships and the exchange of ideas, practitioners, and scholars between both countries.

This collaboration was an enriching learning experience that contributed to professional growth. Antrop-González has travelled to the Dominican Republic five times, and described how previous experiences affected his work. "I felt more confident in my own follow-through due to my additional work experience in the DR. This collaboration has renewed my spirit of urgency to work with teachers as intellectuals in Latin America. I learned that there is a strong desire for popular education in the DR" (2013). McCleer enjoyed building face-to-face as well as virtual friendships and collegial relationships, which have expanded her perspective on global information access. Although García-Febo had collaborated previously on other global initiatives, she was pleasantly surprised at the "hunger" for education demonstrated by participants. It was revealing to engage in lively conversations about professional development and to work with communities to access information to improve health, finances, and overall well-being.

In March 2013, Antrop-Gonzalez and McCleer led a one-week Alternative Spring Break program in Santiago Rodríguez with five Milwaukee students from library and information science, education, and environment studies. The students' diverse perspectives contributed to rich dialogue and peer learning. The group engaged in community projects identified during the February conference, including educational exchanges with Dominican students, assisting with development of the country's first twenty-four-hour educational television channel, and working with teachers to improve the organization and functionality of a school library. The group was also invited to consult with the Universidad Autónoma de Santo Domingo dean of education, who is developing the country's first library and information science degree program.

Project partners continue to promote the initial results of this collaborative project locally, nationally, and internationally. McCleer conducted a doctoral student presentation describing various project components of research, teaching, and service. Four partners presented at the 2013 American Library Association conference in Chicago, communicating best practices of international collaboration. García-Febo shared details at the 2013 International Federation of Library Associations presidential meeting in Mexico, the 2013 German Library Association Conference, as well as at the 2013 Annual Conference of the Association of Caribbean University, Research and Institutional Libraries in Puerto Rico. Partners are currently developing online, custom-designed educational tools, based on an in-depth regional assessment.

CONCLUSIONS

Organizations partnering to support information access in the Dominican Republic have increased their impact and capacity through collaboration. They became aware of intercultural skills that helped them understand diverse populations. Careful planning provided the basis for understanding and respecting each other, which was paramount to the project's success. Joint work with different groups contributed to developing the professional lives of partners and participants. The results of their efforts have been shared at national and international venues, providing others with strategies for replication. Overall, this collaboration positively affects lives in different regions through efforts to support information access by collaborating with local, regional, and international partners.

REFERENCES

Allard, S., Mehra, B., & Quayyum, M. A. (2007). Intercultural leadership toolkit for librarians: Building awareness to effectively serve diverse multicultural populations. *Education Libraries*, 30(1), 5–12.

Asset-Based Community Development Institute. (2009). Retrieved from http://www.abcdinstitute.org/about/founders/.

Cramer, E., & Boyd, J. (2013). The quest for sustainability in international library development: The experience of the Riecken Foundation. *Collaborative Librarianship*, 5(2), 70–81.

Clark, M., & Gomez, R. (2011). Cost and other barriers to public access computing in developing countries. *Proceedings of the 2011 iConference*. Seattle, WA: ACM.

Educere et Curare Foundation. (2013, May 22). Retrieved from http://educere-curare.org/.

Green, M., Moore, H., & O'Brien, J. (2006). *When people care enough to act*. Toronto: Inclusion Press.

McKnight, J., & Kretzmann, J. (1993). *Building communities from the inside out: A path toward finding and mobilizing a community's assets*. Chicago: ACTA.

Mi, M. (2005). Cultural competence for libraries and librarians in health care institutions. *Journal of Hospital Librarianship*, 5(2), 15–31.

Neuman, S. B., Khan, N., & Dondolo, T. (2008). When I give, I own: Building literacy through READ community libraries in Nepal. *The Reading Teacher*, *61*(7), 513–522.

Oficina Nacional de Estadística. (2015, March 26). Composición porcentual de los hogares, por tenencia de servicio de internet, según características geográficas. Retrieved from http://www.one.gob.do/Estadisticas/191/tecnologias-de-la-informacion-y-las-comunicaciones.

Polanco-Almonte, Y. A., & Álvarez Armenteros, C. (2012) Crisis? What crisis? The use of statistics and data for libraries at a turning point—statistics and evaluation. *World Library and Information Congress: 78th IFLA General Conference and Assembly*, Helsinki, Finland.

Satgoor, U., & Schnuer, S. (2005). International partnership, national impact: The South African library leadership project. *IFLA publications*, *116*, 267.

Seibo al Progreso Organization Wisconsin Inc. (2013). Retrieved from https://www.facebook.com/pages/Seibo-al-Progreso-Organization-Wisconsin Inc/193832677322225.

Sharpe, P. A., Greaney, M. L., Lee, P. R., & Royce, S. W. (2000). Assets-oriented community assessment. *Public Health Reports*, *115*(2/3), 205.

United Nations. Population and Vital Statistics Report: Statistical Papers, Series A, Vol. LXVII. (2015, January 1). Retrieved from http://unstats.un.org/unsd/demographic/products/vitstats/Sets/Series_A_2015.pdf.

HOW DO YOU SAY "PENGUIN" IN K'AQCHIKEL?

Promoting Literacy in Guatemala

Stephen E. Stratton

When I first accepted my position at California State University Channel Islands (CI), I was attracted in part by the university's simple mission statement. "Placing students at the center of the educational experience, California State University Channel Islands provides undergraduate and graduate education that facilitates learning within and across disciplines through integrative approaches, emphasizes experiential and service learning, and graduates students with multicultural and international perspectives" (California State University Channel Islands, 2005). As I began work building library collections and services for a new university, which opened in 2002, as well as the Broome Library, which opened in 2008, it quickly became clear that the faculty who had arrived before me took this mission seriously.

We quickly integrated our library mission into the mission of the university: "The John Spoor Broome Library enhances the university's mission through active collaboration with students, faculty, and staff in developing collections, services, information and computer literacy skills." The founding faculty and staff of Broome Library believed what Andrew Dillon, dean of the School of Information at the University of Texas, would later state: "Libraries cannot thrive without aligning their workings directly to the core mission of their host institutions" (Dillon,

2008). Broome Library integrated the service-learning mission through internships and work with our rapidly growing archival collections. We added integrative approaches through our information literacy program, which was built into individual program courses and the educational outcomes of the university.

Given our Hispanic-serving institution status and the diversity of library staff, CI is a multicultural institution. We partnered with faculty to host events during international week, bought and hung the flags of the United Nations in the new building, and built collections around travel and international study programs and courses. However, we still believed we were lacking in direct international experience as library faculty. How, then, could the library better support this fourth mission pillar of the university? How could we bring an international perspective to the Broome Library?

As a start, I became involved with International Federation of Library Associations (IFLA). IFLA is an international, independent, nongovernmental organization. It is the leading international body representing libraries, librarians, and information users around the globe. Being appointed to an IFLA committee introduced me to libraries and librarians from other regions of the world and the work they are doing. Further, I traveled when possible to learn more about libraries in other areas. By traveling with CI faculty on vacations abroad or by providing lectures abroad with them, I was able to gain a global perspective on libraries, librarians, and library users.

In 2010, I was awarded a professional development grant to study Spanish in Guatemala. I had not worked on my Spanish since high school, and there was great need for that skill at CI. Language acquisition studies have shown that spending even brief periods abroad studying a language improves a student's skill in the language (Carroll, 1967). I spent six weeks in Antigua, a small but vibrant city with an immersion language study program. When I was granted a semester-long sabbatical in 2012, I chose to return to Guatemala to continue language study, but also to expand my knowledge of its libraries, to seek information about its suitability as a destination opportunity for CI students, and to support development and growth of libraries in this beautiful country. Both visits combined to provide an exploratory opportunity.

One element of learning language in Guatemala is the opportunity language schools provide to stay in the homes of local families. Homestays have been shown to improve language acquisition in students and provide better cultural awareness of the country than stays in dormitories (Hull & Lemke, 1978). During both trips, I stayed with the same family, an older couple who have an adult son living with them. Living with a family other than your own requires skills such as flexibility, empathy, an acceptance of differences in family interactions, and it also presents the challenges of communicating in another language (Dorn, 2005). Differences in food type and quantity, meal times, and sleeping hours created an initial adjustment period during my first visit.

Antigua is a city of approximately 35,000 people in the highlands of Guatemala. It is a UNESCO World Heritage Site. Spain built the city in 1543 and named it the capital of the Captaincy-General of Guatemala, the colony that covered all of Central America. After an earthquake destroyed the city in 1773, the ruins were left behind and a new capital was built. The ruins are what make Antigua unique, along with other buildings rehabilitated in the Baroque style of the colonial capital. The city is surrounded by three active volcanoes and sits at an altitude of 5,000 feet, keeping a mild climate all year round.

I needed to apply corresponding skills while navigating through Guatemalan society in general. Guatemala is a multicultural country with one official language and twenty-three other nationally recognized languages, twenty-one of them belonging to the Mayan language family. Approximately 40 percent of the population speaks a language other than Spanish at home (Central Intelligence Agency, 2013). Be prepared to accept that you will not always understand the expectations or norms of the numerous cultures represented there. In addition to the variety of Mayan traditions, immigrant groups from Korea and India live in some cities, and a sizeable Garifuna population along the Caribbean coast adds to its multicultural nature.

Guatemala is approximately the size of Pennsylvania. Its population is about 15 million, 50 percent urban and 50 percent rural. Nearly one-third lives in the Guatemala City metropolitan region (Central Intelligence Agency, 2013). The majority of the rest of the population lives in the mountain highlands that range through the central part of the country. Guatemalans under age nineteen make up more than half of the country. The population boom resulted from the end of thirty-six years of civil war, which killed hundreds of thousands of Guatemalans.

Since California State University's chancellor had banned travel of any kind to Mexico (Schmidt, 2013), we needed to identify another location for students to study language and learn about the culture of people immigrating to the region the university serves. CI's Spanish faculty possessed no firsthand knowledge of Guatemala. The library does have a history of coteaching credit-bearing courses with subject faculty about a variety of areas for potential student travel (business, economics, communications, political science). Therefore, my secondary project goals were to learn about libraries, literacy, and available opportunities in Guatemala.

I equipped myself with contact names from librarians who had traveled to Guatemala, as well as those gleaned from professional colleagues from the American Library Association and IFLA. My first trip involved study at the Christian Spanish Academy, the only language school in Antigua fully accredited by the Cervantes Institute, a Spanish governmental agency that accredits language programs around the world. As a result, I became familiar with the region of Antigua and other opportunities available to me and, potentially, to CI students. On my following visit, I selected a language school in Antigua set up to benefit local libraries. Proyecto Bibliotecas Guatemala (Probigua) administers two bookmobiles that travel to small rural villages that otherwise have no access to books, and works to establish and maintain physical libraries in other communities (Probigua, 2011). I also contacted another nongovernmental organization, Child-Aid, which provides direct training to teachers and librarians to improve literacy among students, instill a love of reading, create and support local libraries, and help young readers develop critical thinking skills (Child-Aid, 2013).

FIGURE 9.1. Probigua bibliobus (bookmobile) (Credit: Stephen E. Stratton)

Planning to study for three months in early 2012, I coordinated volunteering in advance with both Probigua and Child-Aid. This was more of a challenge than I anticipated. Emails and phone calls were well received, but I learned later that staff often wait until a person arrives before assigning any volunteer work. Admittedly, I departed for Guatemala not knowing exactly what my volunteer tasks would be. Understandably, since communication is the first challenge to conquer in any country, it's vital to acquire a local cellphone that can receive emails and texts. Although most people don't own a computer, and Wi-Fi connections are sparse or nonexistent in many regions, most Guatemalans own some type of messaging cellphone.

Public libraries are not a common sight in Guatemala. Many libraries open to the public operate as closed-stack facilities that do not lend materials. Several NGOs operate in Guatemala to build or expand library services. Guatemala has the second-lowest adult literacy rate in the Western Hemisphere and a mean completion rate of 4.1 years of schooling for adults, placing it below Haiti in this development measure (United Nations Development Programme, 2013). Rural education and literacy lag far behind levels in urban areas. Fewer than one in ten indigenous children in Guatemala finishes high school. Seventy-five percent of indigenous women cannot read or write in any language (Hallman, 2007). Indigenous Mayan people primarily live in rural areas and use one or more of their languages to communicate in the home and community. The previously discussed demographics and information needs of Guatemalans reflect an ongoing challenge to the two NGOs where I spent time volunteering, but not to potential volunteers. Because the need is exceptional, opportunities for librarians, library students, or interested student groups are wide and varied.

Traveling one day with John van Keppel, local director of Child-Aid, I learned how I could contribute. We visited several school and library sites around the central highlands, where I observed a teacher-training session in Campo Verde de Santa Lucia Utatlán. Guatemalan teachers and librarians must have graduated high school to qualify for their positions. While this level of education far exceeds the mean, it still often leaves teachers and librarians underprepared. Child-Aid works with local communities to build these educators' skills. Local educators with knowledge of Mayan languages conduct these literacy-skills trainings.

Many Guatemalan schools require some instruction in the local indigenous language, and some teachers speak these languages better than Spanish. Most instruction is in Spanish, as required by the government, while some schools choose to offer some English. I learned that

Child-Aid hosts work groups from the United States that assist rural villages by building, maintaining, repairing, and improving schools and libraries.

Erin Conway, Child-Aid's director of training and curriculum, helped start a library in the village of Santa Catarina Palopó (located in Sololá department, the government equivalent of a U.S. state). Her foundation, named *Weave, Hope*, helps underwrite the local librarian's salary as well as purchase books. I choose to spend a week cataloging books with Ana Pascuala Lopez, the librarian at Ru K'ux Na'oj ("Heart of Knowledge" in the K'aqchikel language) in Santa Catarina Palopó. Lopez had been cataloging books by hand on spreadsheets created by Conway that were then entered in a computer spreadsheet. Neither Ana nor the library had a computer. The one-room library served as a gathering place for students before or after school.

Child-Aid trained Lopez in teaching and literacy methods, and she performs outreach to classrooms at the local school. She also encourages teachers to bring classes to the library for story time. Lopez posed ques-

FIGURE 9.2. Santa Catarina Palopó from the hillside toward Lago de Atitlán (Lake Atitlán) (Credit: Stephen E. Stratton)

tions during story time to encourage critical thinking in the students. Cataloging these books would help Ana have an accurate record of library materials, so she could begin lending books to students.

I had to record materials in languages with which I was unfamiliar. I have experience with Spanish, but reading K'aqchikel, K'iche', or Tz'utujil was new, and I was unfamiliar with use of the apostrophe to represent glottal stops. I generally had to seek Ana's assistance about which language I was encountering and how to proceed. The challenge was quickly evident in building and maintaining a paper catalog or a catalog on a spreadsheet accessible only to Lopez. Much time was spent helping students find books they wanted to read or to have read to them.

Understandably, it was unusual adjusting to a small town where Spanish is the second language. Knowing I would never understand K'aqchikel and wouldn't have Internet access gave me a lot of time to simply observe and be observed. Interacting with children at the library brought me the most conversation. A young student and I had joint vocabulary lessons, as he was studying names of animals for his

FIGURE 9.3. Ru K'ux Na'oj, the library at Santa Catarina Palopó (Credit: Stephen E. Stratton)

homework. He would query me about names of animals in English and I would respond, then ask him their names in K'aqchikel. We conversed in Spanish, exchanging words for dog, duck, cat, horse—and then came penguin. He asked, "Como se dice pingüino en ingles?" to which I responded, "Penguin." "Como se dice pingüino en K'aqchikel?" I returned the question. He thought for a moment and was silent. Then he told me in Spanish, "We don't have penguins in K'aqchikel." We both laughed, but it was true: there was no word for penguin because there are no penguins within the range of the K'aqchikel people. This simple exchange gave me a better understanding of this boy trying to place his culture and town within the world, but it also helped me understand him with empathy.

My experience working in the indigenous community of Santa Catarina Palopó increased my involvement in IFLA with the Special Interest Group (SIG) on Indigenous Matters. I had the opportunity to represent this group at the second Joint Conference of Librarians of Color, presenting a poster session about the activities of the IFLA SIG, as well as librarians around the world working in indigenous areas, indigenous librarian gatherings, and the concerns of indigenous peoples related to libraries and providing information. As an outsider in this professional world, trying to represent Guatemala or indigenous people, I will always be learning.

I had a wonderful time traveling through Guatemala with Rigoberto Zamora Charuc, the founder of Probigua. Although I did not spend as much time volunteering with Probigua, I enjoyed the opportunity to see different libraries throughout the country. I journeyed to Pueblo Nuevo Tiquisate in the south to deliver books to the public library. It had a computer lab established by a Gates Foundation grant, and provides regular computer courses for local residents.

I witnessed the celebration of International Day of the Book (April 23) in the town of Chicacao. This was much grander than I had imagined, as all the students in the area schools turned out for speeches, entertainers, and music in the central park. Several people donated books to the public library. The International Day of the Book is widely acknowledged in Guatemalan schools and libraries.

I also visited the bibliobus (bookmobile) and provided story time to children in San Lorenzo Tejar. San Lorenzo, a small village outside Antigua, has no public or school library. As an academic librarian, I don't often conduct story time or read aloud. I'm afraid my skills were a bit rusty, as I put one child to sleep that day. However, I was able to

FIGURE 9.4. Storytime at the library (Credit: Stephen E. Stratton)

entertain another youngster with several stories. After he left, I learned that he didn't attend school regularly because his family needs him for farming. I was moved by his interest in trying to read along with me.

Once I returned to CI, I wanted to maintain regular practice in developing Spanish skills, as well as the momentum toward creating opportunities for our students, and continue relationships I developed with library organizations in Guatemala.

I started by sharing photos and speaking with colleagues. Of course, Facebook provided this opportunity during the project. Further, I offered presentations, first within the library, then to the campus, and most recently to community groups interested in learning more about Guatemala. To respond to the diverse questions I received, I resolved to read more extensively about Guatemala's history and culture. One of our librarians suggested gifting duplicate materials to Probigua. The local Mexican consulate had donated a collection of curricular materials with many duplicates. We boxed them up and shipped them for Probigua to distribute as needed. However, shipping books abroad is expensive, because materials can only be sent by airmail. Library foundation funds paid for this. Still, of the ten boxes shipped to Probigua, only eight arrived, underscoring problems with the Guatemalan postal service. Future shipments will be handled through private carriers to guarantee that they arrive.

Designing and delivering a course for students has been more problematic. Discipline faculty have varied interests and none currently focuses on Guatemala in their research. However, the director of the Center for International Affairs has assisted me in developing a course focusing on libraries and literacy in Guatemala, which will be submitted for funding this coming year. The student fees board may provide funding to facilitate students traveling to Guatemala at reduced cost. Study-abroad trips generally involve groups of about twenty students and stays of a week to ten days. Since these courses are offered through general university studies, they are electives and don't depend on support from any particular program or department. If approved, I may have the chance to travel with a group of students as part of the campus's first trip to Guatemala. I hope that the itinerary will be enhanced by my Guatemalan contacts.

As I speak about Guatemala, libraries, and books, other professional opportunities continue to arise. This year I'm planning to speak to the Rotaract Club. The club's advisors at Broome Library report that students are interested in projects in Central America and in libraries in particular. This corresponds well to the original funding of Probigua's bookmobiles, which were older Bluebird school buses provided by Rotary clubs in the U. S. and Canada.

International librarianship is more than a one-time adventure. I have achieved a sense of connectedness to the work of Ana, Ru K'ux Na'oj, Probigua, and the librarians and teachers I met in Guatemala. Although several other foundations or NGOs work with libraries in Guatemala, I am adamant about supporting these groups in any way I can. Whether accomplished through continued book donations, securing funds from family and friends, or planning a return trip to Guatemala, this project has become an avocation enriching both my personal and professional life.

REFERENCES

California State University Channel Islands. (2005). CI mission statement. Retrieved from http://www.csuci.edu/about/mission.htm.

California State University Channel Islands. (n.d.). GE goals and outcomes. Retrieved from http://www.csuci.edu/provost/ge-taskforce/goalsandoutcomes.htm.

Carroll, J. B. (1967). Foreign language proficiency levels attained by language majors near graduation from college. *Foreign Language Annals*, *1*(1), 131–151.

Central Intelligence Agency. (2013). *Guatemala*. Retrieved from https://www.cia.gov/library/publications/the-world-factbook/geos/gt.html.

Child-Aid. (2013). *The power of literacy*. Retrieved from http://child-aid.org/.

Dillon, A. (2008, August). *Accelerating learning and discovery: Refining the role of academic libraries*. Retrieved from http://www.clir.org/pubs/reports/pub142/dillon.html.

Dorn, G. a.-K. (2005). Intercultural skills: A guide to working with other cultures. Retrieved from http://www.in languages.com/documents/Interculturalskills.pdf.

Hallman, K. S. (2007, June). *Assessing the multiple disadvantages of Mayan girls: The effects of gender, ethnicity, poverty, and residence on education in Guatemala*. Retrieved from www.avivara.org:http://www.avivara.org/images/Assessing_the_multiple_disadvantages_of_Mayan_girls.pdf.

Hull, W. F., IV, and Lemke, W. H., Jr. (1978). Research findings and administrative implications for off-campus higher education. *International Review of Education*, *24*(1): 53–64.

Probigua. (2011, November 11). *Who we are*. Retrieved from http://www.probigua.org/files/en/index-1.html.

Schmidt, E. (2013, March 13). CSU chancellor removes study abroad to Mexico ban. Retrieved from http://www.daily49er.com/news/csu-chancellor-removes-study-abroad-to-mexico-ban-1.2817874#.UawD-WRRgt0.

United Nations Development Programme. (2013). *International Human Development Indicators*. Retrieved from Data Explorer: http://hdr.undp.org/en/data/explorer/.

RECOMMENDED READING

Bell, E. (2010). *Antigua Guatemala: The city and its heritage*. 5th ed. Antigua: Antigua Tours.

Corrado, R. (2014). El Lustrador. Guatemala City: Editorial Palo de Hormigo.

Grandin, G., Levenson, D. T., and Ogelsby, E. (Eds.). (2011). *The Guatemala reader*. Durham, NC: Duke University Press.

INTERNATIONAL PARTNERSHIPS

BUILDING CAPACITY FOR INTERNATIONAL LIBRARIANSHIP THROUGH INTERCULTURAL PROFESSIONAL PARTNERSHIPS AND CIVIL SOCIETY OUTREACH IN TANZANIA

Chantal Phillips

I recently had the pleasure of serving with a team of academics in Canada and Tanzania on an international project, Building Civil Society Capacity for Poverty Reduction. Canada's Huron University College established a partnership with the University of Dar es Salaam's Institute of Development Studies to reinvigorate their curriculum. Graduate programs were redesigned and expanded to engage civil society organizations and provide graduate students with service learning experiences. A pilot study on information access facilitated fieldwork and the engagement of librarians in Canada and Tanzania by investigating information needs at the village level. This rural and remote case study highlighted the participatory processes necessary for collaboration between academics, civil society organizations, and community members.

This project renewed facilities and collections for graduate students and a small district public library, an effort that included introducing Swahili language materials. This chapter will review some of the project design strategies, which emphasize participation in order to strengthen outcomes.

The university in Dar es Salaam and faculty from Canada have been working for over ten years on this partnership. Tanzania's poverty-reduction strategy includes next-generation solutions. To reduce poverty, youth must be educated and graduates must be able to participate fully as citizens. Librarianship is part of the task of creating a civil society with access to information about strengthening poverty reduction strategies and increasing participation.

In its Vision 2025, Tanzania describes itself as a middle-income country in which absolute poverty has been eradicated. At present, however, Tanzanians still struggle with many challenges, including food security. According to the Global Hunger Index 2013, more people are undernourished in Tanzania than in any East African country except Burundi. Developing access to information and resources for civil society is part of the government's strategy of reaching the United Nations Millennium Development Goals. Tanzania's multiethnic and multilingual society has been a beacon of predominantly peaceful democratic traditions, allowing for elections and political administrations that have not faced the upheavals of some of its East African neighbors.

However, the largely rural poor have not shared in recent growth and continue to live without adequate access to education, food security, and healthcare. The university partners are determined to work with rural Tanzanians regardless of language or ethnicity, and introduce graduate student researchers to alleviate some problems with access to information.

PARTICIPATORY DEVELOPMENT

No matter how hard we try to shed cultural baggage, the unfortunate reality about working with libraries outside North America and Europe is that a colonial past often hampers good working relationships. Creating a framework that bolsters strong partnerships, joint responsibilities, and clear and equally shared delegation of authority goes a long way toward establishing effective project teams. This is always the case, but is particularly useful when partners with cultural, linguistic, and historical differences are trying to establish a locally sustainable program.

For example, the advisory committee in the donor country should not decide which equipment is best suited for the project, just because purchases can be made and shipped to the partner. Equipment budgets and specifications should be the result of a local dialogue, which determines the long-term sustainability of maintaining facilities, equipment, and collections.

A framework of responsibilities can be developed from the start through a variety of tools, such as Results-Based Management, a project-management process employed by large organizations such as the Canadian International Development Agency and the Canadian government. This moves work objectives away from specifics, such as counting books

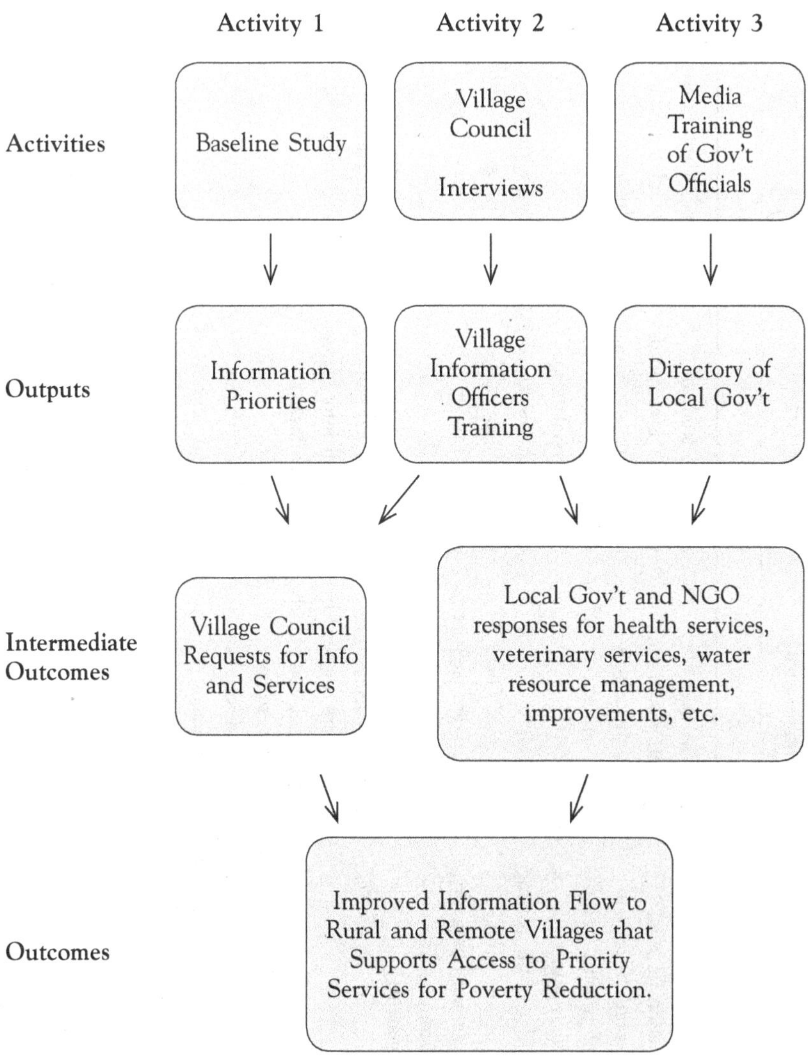

FIGURE 10.1. Flow chart logic model

Table 10.1. Results Based Management

Profile	*Logic Model*	*Measurement*	*Evaluation*	*Reporting*
Improve access to information for rural and remote villagers in areas of priority, such as improving maternal and child health, getting access to education, better animal husbandry, and water resource management.	Rationale: Better information can improve decision-making in health, agriculture, and education. Assumption: There is local, relevant support to address priority needs in district government and local NGO sector. Print resources are not read by most people, don't reach village government offices, and aren't in local languages. Resources: Cellphones and local government officials can provide access to better information.	A baseline study of villagers to assess needs and restraints as identified by the locals. Measure population, identify schools, clinics, vet and ag extension offices, and other supports. Village council meetings to establish information needs of villagers. Interviews with key local officials and elders to identify priorities, threats to progress, and opportunities.	A journal of activities to measure and report on Village Information Officers. A meeting with Village officials to review actions taken on priority issues. An assessment with local government officials on solutions provided for priorities.	Midterm review and annual reports, and final report deadlines.

added to the collection, to more substantial results, such as improved access to information and promotion of a reading culture.

Some key considerations in developing the project and action plan are:

> *When?*
> Is your trip to the project area planned for the rainy season when roads are impassable, or for holidays when key people are away?
>
> *Who?*
> Have you surveyed only those who showed up, or do you plan to talk to those who are sick at home, who are unable to travel due to childcare responsibilities, or who speak a dialect but don't read the official language?
>
> *How?*
> Are you making assumptions about who does what in this community? Perhaps men and women have different ideas about this topic, based on different responsibilities at home and work. Can you employ a process that encourages gender disaggregation of results?

Techniques such as meeting with community leaders to learn local issues and prioritize needs can inform a project by tying it to existing realities. Dividing up women and men into small groups for discussion, and valuing youth, elders, and children can create a fuller picture of the community. Using groups to create maps of a place such as a campus or village can highlight issues that are important to people who are not fluent in literate cultures that demand written submissions and reports to create background documents. There are many participation strategies to choose from, and they all help form relationships, build a strong base for future work, and increase options when unforeseen circumstances require project plans to be redirected.

Tight or nonexistent acquisition budgets in many African libraries can lead to decisions based not on collection or user assessment, but simply on lack of materials. Full shelves are better than empty ones, aren't they? Using input from baseline research and other participatory processes can lead to better decisions than filling shelves with second-hand materials cast off from North American libraries. This project developed a selection tool every year and used it in academic and public library systems to support project-funded acquisitions. In our village case study, cellular telecommunications afforded easier access to government officials and information, thereby enabling more effective decision-making. The fact that virtually everyone has access to phones and is familiar with their use removes barriers print-based resources create where most citizens are not literate in the official language of government.

CULTURAL ANALYSIS IN THE PROJECT ENVIRONMENT

The context of a library project is always unique, and skills related to an environmental scan or a SWOT analysis (strengths, weaknesses, opportunities, and threats) are extremely useful. At the initial stages, the team or project leader should be able to draw an accurate picture of the project context. We developed the initial project documents for a large grant with a team of academics, including librarians and faculty, who were equally balanced between Tanzanian nationals and Canadians with international experience.

Following that, a baseline study was developed and implemented with the fieldwork of Tanzanian faculty and graduate students. They made multiple trips and developed case studies, resulting in selection of the best pilot sites, which had support of local leaders and municipal government. Locals translated in this trilingual, multiethnic project environment. This heavy investment in building a collaborative environment was validated over and over as local officials demonstrated support for decisions and project sustainability.

Key results of working with local leaders:

1. Local elders identified priority information needs, highlighting current problems with water, animals, children, and health.

2. Local elders allowed project staff into council meetings.

3. Local elders appointed Village Information Officers, giving them access to council meetings and the right to speak.

Without these initial meetings with leaders, there would have been less information about the type of data needed to support strong communities and fewer opportunities for project volunteers, such as Village Information Officers, to be integrated into decision making.

Given our choice to work with poor and rural Maasai villagers in the first case study, it was important to validate their cultural traditions and apply successful information-gathering practices from their cultural heritage. The Village Information Officer model was based on the traditional role that young men run from *boma* (homestead) to *boma* spreading information. The use of a model representing a successful cultural practice strengthened the sustainability of the collaboration and laid the foundation for work that was easy to translate between three working languages and cultures. There was no need to explain the reason for using young people as a source of information or validating the place of the Village Information Officer in local council meetings. The new responsibilities were a good fit with old ideas about gathering information and spreading it in the community.

The analysis of gender roles within the local environment helped identify differences between women and men in the project environment. The creation of specific groups to request input from both men and women helped clarify differences in their information priorities. They also adopted traditional models of separate women's and men's councils. The importance of stressing the need for both a man and woman to be information officers from each village was justified by both cultural practices and differences stated in the baseline study between women and men. For example, women retrieve water and fuel wood—they are more concerned with water and forest management. Men, on the other hand, prioritize livestock and veterinarian services, and are concerned with grazing rights and market sale of animals. These different priorities are equally important and were represented in the life of the project due to the explicit goal of using gender analysis as a tool.

LOCAL CONTENT

Relevant local content is the cornerstone of a successful library project. The challenges of access to good-quality local information resources remain, whether we consider books or digital objects. While we supported use of oral culture in one case study, we purchased books for the second case study to support a small district public library in Baganoyo. Despite the fact that books disintegrate rapidly in the humid coastal climate, we determined that it was important to support local curriculum and purchase textbooks for public borrowing. With the support of local book distributors, we selected and purchased the books.

Several Canadian organizations are strong supporters of development of the local book chain in the Global South. CODE Canada works with a Tanzanian NGO, Children's Book Project. Through this connection, I learned how local authors are involved in award competitions for new books. The winning entries judged by local experts are published and distributed to school libraries. This ensures that quality books are promoted and that new local authors have a chance to thrive where few opportunities exist for advancing a reading culture for adults who are often unable to purchase reading materials in their mother tongue.

CHALLENGES OF COLLABORATION

Many challenges of teamwork are evident in the collaboration required for international projects. Some of these are mired in the realities of poverty and inequality. Creating a project framework that anticipates challenges is fundamental. International colleagues in the Global South may not have access to credit cards, while travel to North America requires credit card transactions for tickets, accommodations, transportation, and numerous other logistical details. For starters, try not to assume that your colleagues are able to share various financial aspects of the project.

With repeated requests for rigorous reporting, we frequently transmit negative stereotypes about lack of financial accountability in countries of the Global South. This can affect project outcomes. The relative nonexistence of receipts for goods, invoices for sales, and itemized records for contracts and labor costs is frequently poorly understood by those accustomed to more complex business practices. It would never occur to most people to question whether the project team has differing values and constraints placed on them by financial transactions and other differences in the local business environment.

Trying to comprehend different financial practices and values makes it easier to reach compromises, fulfilling needs for accurate reporting and outcomes. Not sure whether the carpenter is charging too much? Don't use a foreigner to obtain estimates. A local project leader will employ the budget wisely if there is an incentive to get the most for their project and they feel ownership and responsibility to their fellow villagers or colleagues.

Is there generally a lack of paper receipts for work, and are there no time sheets for labor charges? First, determine whether it is best to bring receipt books or create logbooks for staff and volunteers to track charges and labor expenses. Perhaps a customary practice already exists that will work best if the project can adapt it to the reporting requirements. Try to be explicit about money matters from the start and discuss issues as they arise.

Governance structures and processes can reinforce strengths and weaknesses in project environments. If the balance of the project team is well matched, then the partnership can respond when challenges arise. Locals may provide alternatives that work in the real world. Foreign nationals can bring alternative suggestions into the project to test and trial.

Time expended in sound project design and balanced team composition pays off down the road. Likewise, the language and materials the project operates can either increase or reduce participation. Is there a common language? Can time be taken for translation and interpretation during meetings, or is it more effective to have bilingual and trilingual team members facilitate cross-cultural encounters? Promotion of plain language usage and support for oral cultures and multilingual resources are additional tools to increase the number of people who can actively support and participate. Closing the door to multiple languages decreases the breadth of a project beyond the teams' boundaries.

After the project achieves its stated mission, issues can still remain to be ironed out. This requires practice on the ground and review of what has been implemented. Despite our best efforts to reach out and support a district library with books that matched local classroom reading lists, we still discovered that although the books were cataloged, they were not on display in the library. Obviously, a crucial set of questions hadn't been posed. Possibly they feared that books would be stolen, perhaps it was perceived that they should only be displayed when students visited. There may have been other rational factors to restrict access that we never considered. An open dialogue can arise only if project partners believe their concerns and ideas are listened to respectfully. Clearly, we hadn't spent enough time in the library to become aware of them. Once we requested that books be put on display, local librarians were happy to comply.

With our local partners, we produced a broad array of project outcomes:

1. *Capacity development:* We strengthened the capacity of University of Dar es Salaam to offer gender-equitable programming on civil society and poverty reduction for students and civil society organizations through a curriculum renewal process. New programs were developed and implemented, new courses are being offered, and students are gaining field experience working with local groups.

2. *Information resources and services development:* We increased, sustained, and provided equitable access to gender-inclusive information on civil society and poverty reduction, primarily through the library of the University of Dar es Salaam (USDM) and its Graduate Resource Centre of the Institute for Development Studies. Over 300 books were donated and cataloged for student access in the main library, a renovated graduate student center, and the district library of Bagamoyo.

3. *Outreach:* A successful case study engaged Village Information Officers and local officials in responding to information needs in remote and rural villages. A partnership with one district library led to better access to local language materials for students after more than sixty books were acquired and cataloged.

This international partnership was a success by several measures. One key indicator is the strengthening of ties. There is no doubt that this will lead to other successful collaborations. Partners in both countries will entertain new proposals to continue collaboration. We hope that these results will inspire others to initiate new projects.

Tanzanian graduate students, a multiethnic and multilingual group, and undergraduates from Canada were integral to the project's attributes. They permitted work on the ground to be carried out as planned, managing all the inevitable bumps along the way. The completion of two master's degrees and support of three PhD candidates were additional outcomes. The fact that over half the Canadian students stayed or returned to work in Tanzania confirms that these aspects of service learning are effective means of professional development.

Development of this undertaking through a lengthy partnership and engagement process assured its outcome. It suggests an alternative to top-down models of collaboration across borders, which are frequently driven by tight deadlines and external indicators for success. The lasting impact within the university through the curriculum renewal process and strengthening of library facilities and collections is broadly shared and continues to produce rewards for students. Lastly, thanks to solid relationships between graduate students and villagers, Village Information Officers demonstrated a positive model for information access between local government officials and local leaders. Undoubtedly, future collaborations will enhance our strong and deep ties, which bind us together despite the distance.

REFERENCES

Braman, S. (2009). Theorizing the impact of IT on library-state relations in Information Technology. In G. J. Leckie & J. E. Buschman (Eds.), *Librarianship: A new critical approach*, pp. 105–125. Westport, CT: Libraries Unlimited, 2009.

Byrne, A. (1999, November 4). *Libraries and democracy*. World Library and Information Congress, Stockholm, Sweden: International Federation of Library Associations. Retrieved from http://archive.ifla.org/faife/papers/others/byrne3.htm.

Chambua, S. E., & Mongula, B. (2009). *Building civil society capacity for poverty reduction: A report of the baseline study carried out in Monduli, January 2009*. Institute of Development Studies, University of Dar es Salaam.

Golding, P., & Murdock, G. (1986). Unequal information: Access and exclusion in the new communication marketplace. In M. Ferguson (Ed.), *New communication technologies and the public interest: Comparative perspectives on policy and research*, pp. 71–83). Beverly Hills, CA: Sage Publications.

Maranz, D. (2001). *African friends and money matters: Observations from Africa*. Dallas, TX: SIL International.

Phillips, C., Varpatolai, A., & Roks, M. (2013). *North-South international education partnerships: Two Canadian projects with Tanzania*. Retrieved from http://hdl.handle.net/10214/6369.

Pieterse, J. N. (1997). Multiculturalism and museums: Discourse about others in the age of globalization. *Theory, Culture & Society*, *14*(4), 123–146.

Sey, Araba, and Fellows, M. *Literature review on the impact of public access to information and communication technologies*. CIS Working Paper No. 6. Seattle, WA: Information School, University of Washington. 2009.

Tostensen, A., Tvedten, I., & Vaa, M. (2001). The urban crisis, governance and associational life. In A. Tostensen, I. Tvedten, & M. Vaa (Eds.), *Associational life in African cities: Popular responses to the urban crisis*, pp. 7–26. Uppsala, Finland: Nordic Africa Institute,.

Vainio-Mattila, A., Phillips, C., Mongula, B., & Nkhoma-Wamunza, A. (2010). Democracy, literacy and poverty: Can text messages bring the academic library to African leaders? *Partnership: The Canadian Journal of Library and Information Practice and Research*. 5(2).

PARTNERING IN INTERNATIONAL LIBRARY DEVELOPMENT

Lubuto Library Partners, Zambia Library Service, and Zambia's Ministry of Education

Elizabeth Cramer

The Lubuto Library Partners (LLP) is an international library development organization that provides educational and personal development opportunities to individuals and communities in sub-Saharan African countries, beginning in Zambia, where its model is being developed. LLP works in partnership with nonprofit, professional, and governmental organizations to construct libraries based on traditional architecture, provide book collections and information and communication technology, and offer services and programs that enhance learning and self-expression. LLP serves as an advocate for vulnerable children and teens by creating an inclusive and welcoming environment, and through educating library staff, teachers, and community volunteers about the special needs of this demographic. Jane Meyers, a professional librarian with thirty-five years' experience living and working in Africa, founded the Lubuto Library Partners in 2005.

The Republic of Zambia is located in south central Africa; the city of Lusaka is its capital. Zambia's current population is 15 million people, with a life expectancy of fifty-eight years; 60.5 percent of Zambians live below the national poverty level (World Bank, 2015). In 2013, it was reported that 12.5 percent of adults between the ages of fifteen and forty-nine are HIV-positive, and the mortality rate for children under five is 8.9 percent (Europa Publications Limited, 2015). In 2013, Zambia's gross national income was $1,480 per capita, with an estimated 60 percent working in agriculture. Attendance in primary education is mandatory and in 2012, 94 percent of children between the ages of seven and fourteen attended school. Attendance at secondary school (fourteen to nineteen years old) was 46 percent. The adult literacy rate in 2010 was reported at 71 percent (Europa Publications Limited, 2015).

LLP has established two libraries in Lusaka, Zambia, and in 2013 began construction of its third library in a rural community in Zambia's Southern Province. The Lubuto Library Partners model has been developed over years of direct interaction with beneficiaries. LLP has consulted directly with Zambia's Ministry of Education, Science, Vocational Training and Early Education (MESVTEE), including the Zambia Library Service (ZLS) at every stage of development. A Memoir of Understanding between LLP and the ministry was signed in 2008, naming LLP as a national partner in providing literacy and library services to Zambia's orphans and vulnerable children. This Memoir of Understanding complements national plans to ensure equitable access to educational resources and mandates LLP to provide leadership in establishing standards of good library practice to improve the quality of education in Zambia.

FIGURE 11.1. Three traditional structures that comprise the LLP library at Ngwerere School (Credit: Jane Kinney Meyers)

Since mid-2011, LLP has worked extensively with ZLS to plan the national scale-up and integration of the Lubuto Library Partners model into national library services. ZLS envisions LLP libraries built adjacent to its existing provincial libraries, which currently do not serve children effectively. Like all LLP libraries, the new libraries would provide book collections, technology, targeted programs, and services to the children and youth of the area, with a special focus on vulnerable children. LLP is working with the Zambian government to mobilize funds from both internal and external sources to establish and operate these libraries. Under its formal agreement with the Zambian government, the MESVTEE has ultimate ownership of and responsibility for the LLP libraries, including staffing and operational costs. LLP will provide ongoing in-service training in library services for children and youth to library staff, and train and provide tools for monitoring and evaluating the library's collections and services. In addition, LLP will work directly with library staff and ZLS to plan and schedule library programming and establish effective outreach programs, particularly to out-of-school youth.

The relationship between Lubuto Library Partners and the Zambia Library Service is noteworthy due to the extent of collaboration. The sustainable development of the ZLS/LLP requires work and dedication from both partners to secure funding and to establish a cadre of librarians to work at children's libraries with an emphasis on services for vulnerable youth. If this initiative proves successful, LLP libraries will serve children and youth throughout Zambia, build capacity for children's librarianship, and further raise awareness among government officials and other stakeholders of the benefits of libraries as learning and community centers with a measurable impact. To better understand the benefits and challenges of this partnership's endeavor, the author interviewed individuals specialized in library education, international library development, and libraries in sub-Saharan Africa. Interviewees include Jane Meyers, founder of Lubuto Library Partners; Robinson Bwato, chief librarian of the Zambia Library Service; Benson Njobvu, head of Library and Information Studies at the University of Zambia (UNZA); Stacy Langner, regional program director at Lubuto Library Partners; Mary Wagner, professor emeritus of the School of Library and Information Science, St. Catherine University, and Fulbright scholar who worked in Lusaka, Zambia, in 2010; and Peter Lor, professor in the Department of Information Science at University of Pretoria, 2005–2008 secretary general of the International Federation of Library Associations and member of the Lubuto Library Partners Advisory Board.

IMPORTANCE OF ZAMBIA GUIDING DEVELOPMENT EFFORTS

Many scholars question if NGOs are actually serving the needs of the partner countries or have fallen into a trap of serving their own needs and the desires of the donors (Afwerki, 1997). LLP realizes the importance of understanding reality as perceived by the developing country partner. Meyers emphasizes that "understanding anything about international development relates to trying to see the world through the eyes of the people that you're working with. And that's not an easy thing" (J. K. Meyers, personal communication, January 8, 2012). Library development organizations need to identify the library authority within the developing country and work with this authority body. In the case of Zambian libraries, this is the ZLS, as part of MESVTEE.

In addition to working with ZLS, LLP includes a number of nationals within its structure. The founding member of the LLP Advisory Board is a leading representative of Zambia's culture and arts communi-

FIGURE 11.2. Eleni Coromvli (LLP Regional Program Director), Robinson Bwato and Sharon Munshya of Zambia Library Service, and Jane Meyers (Credit: Jane Kinney Meyers)

ties, having served as chairman of the National Arts Council. Another board member is one of the country's business and civic leaders, who previously served on the National Anti-Corruption Commission. LLP never goes to a significant meeting with government officials without a Zambian representative. Meyers explains, "These are people on whom I rely to know exactly how to deal with the government on particular issues that I'm not familiar with or that simply their communications between each other [are] more direct and more accurate in representing each side's views better" (J. K. Meyers, personal communication, January 8, 2012). Meyers realizes that in official discussions with the government and other stakeholders, the respected country members representing LLP carry more weight than she does.

Lor finds LLP's approach to working with Zambians and the government of the Republic of Zambia to be crucial and very admirable. According to Lor, too many times well-intentioned outsiders establish libraries and fail to collaborate with local authorities or library professionals. Once the development program leaves the country to return home, the libraries fail to thrive because they have never taken root in the community. Lor admires the way Meyers has taken the long-term view, working to build her relationship with the Zambia Library Service.

STRIVE TO MEET THE DEVELOPMENT GOALS OF THE COUNTRY

To ensure that the community values the benefits of the project, donors are advised to align aid specifically with the development strategy and priorities of the developing country (OECD, 2005). LLP, ZLS, and MESVTEE recognize the Millennium Development Goals (MDGs) formed by the United Nations as primary goals of the partnership. These goals include providing universal primary education, eradicating extreme poverty and hunger, employing youth, and improving expertise in technology (United Nations, 2010). This agreement is written into the Memoir of Understanding, stating that LLP and the Ministry will work together to attain the objectives of the MDGs by building libraries that target disadvantaged children, promoting libraries in conjunction with the ZLS, and collaborating to promote literacy and library services.

A recent study by Electronic Information for Libraries (EIFL), "Perception of Public Libraries in Africa" (2011), reveals interview data concerning African libraries, recognition of potential benefits from public libraries, and support for additional allocation of resources to library development. The study covered six African countries—Ethiopia,

Ghana, Kenya, Tanzania, Uganda, and Zimbabwe—and gathered data through interviews with community members, public librarians, and local and national government officials. The majority of those interviewed viewed public libraries as mostly small and underfunded—places that supplied books and a place to study, as opposed to supplying digital technologies or community development services. But the majority also recognized that if public libraries received sufficient funding, libraries could help achieve development goals (EIFL, 2011).

Bwato believes that the partnership between LLP and ZLS meets the Millennium Development Goals in that LLP provides needed attention to children excluded by the formal school system, as well as meets the needs of orphans and vulnerable children. Lor stresses the fact that libraries can support all the MDGs, but they support them somewhat indirectly. Libraries can play an important role in disseminating information that leads to lower infant mortality or improved educational outcomes, but it is difficult to attribute the percentage of improvement that originates from libraries.

INTERNATIONAL LIBRARY DEVELOPMENT LEADERS NEED TO POSSESS PROFESSIONAL LIBRARY CREDENTIALS

Leaders of international library development initiatives need to question what they bring to developing countries as outsiders. A fundamental tenet for LLP is that library development advisers need to be library professionals with appropriate credentials to successfully engage with another country. Often international library development initiatives are directed by nonprofessionals. LLP questions the value of their expertise, especially when they are offering advice to professional librarians in the partner country. As Langner states, "It would be patronizing for us to say we were building capacity of the Zambia Library Service if none of us had any background in information science. We can't teach people something we aren't experts in" (S. Langner, personal communication, June 21, 2013).

CHALLENGE: MOBILIZING FINANCIAL RESOURCES FOR LUBUTO LIBRARY PARTNERS

Some scholars question the possible success of sustainable development in Africa due to economic realities. If some governments are unable or unwilling to commit domestic resources, programs will suffer without continued foreign funds and expertise (Easterly, 2006). Withdrawal of financial aid has been proven to lead to decline in services in development projects (Kremer & Miguel, 2008; Ravichandran & Rajashree, 2007).

LLP is working with ZLS and MESVTEE in a variety of ways to mobilize resources for the creation and support of sustainable libraries. As with many developing countries, Zambia's national budget comes partially from tax revenue, but is also subsidized by international donors. Since LLP and the Zambian government are working together to create libraries that support national development goals, government representatives are well prepared to speak with international donors about the need for financial resources to support libraries.

LLP also serves as an expert advisor in mobilizing additional funding, always with the knowledge and participation of the Zambian government. It is vital that LLP work in conjunction with the government for two main reasons: major donors want to support projects that have government buy-in, plus MESVTEE owns the libraries and is responsible for their management. When Langner wrote a recent proposal to Comic Relief for donations to help with construction of the next LLP library, it was necessary to clarify how LLP would work within government structures to carry out the work.

Bwato recognizes the importance of mobilizing financial resources. The first step is to increase the Zambian government's interest in, appreciation for, and knowledge of children's libraries. Successful advocacy would result in an act from the National Assembly of Parliament securing direct funding for libraries. The challenge is that support of libraries may not be in the best interest of politicians, because it is not directly addressed in the MDGs or the country's development goals. Politicians view other issues, such as improved schools and hospitals, as more effective campaign platforms (Bukenya, 2009).

Njobvu and Wagner speak highly of the LLP and ZLS partnership, but have reservations about receiving funding from the Zambian government. As part of his research, Njobvu recently completed a tour of forty-eight schools in five provinces of Zambia. Only two of these schools had anything resembling a library for the students. He uses this as an example to illustrate the lack of government resources available to support any kind of library, whether academic, public, or children's. Mary Wagner believes it will be a challenge for LLP and ZLS to secure funds in the face of competing priorities such as food, shelter, and employment.

Lor believes low prioritization of libraries is a worldwide phenomenon. There is never enough money, even in the United States and United Kingdom, where hundreds of libraries or branches have been closed in the last year or two as the result of austerity measures. He believes it is a matter of making your case and getting yourself a bit higher up on the priority list, something LLP and ZLS are currently working to achieve.

CHALLENGE: TRAINING LIBRARIANS TO WORK IN LLP LIBRARIES

Developing strong leaders and committed staff is a major concern in the success of sustainable development. In addressing capacity building, the Paris Declaration recognizes the importance of strengthening human resources, and stresses that building capacity is primarily the role of the partner country with support from the donor (OECD, 2005). There is little professional training for children's librarianship in Africa. Library and information science curricula tend to focus on technology and other academic specializations (Ochalla & Bothma, 2007). Njobvu explains that currently the UNZA Library and Information Science program does not focus on teaching skills for working in specific types of libraries such as school, public, or academic. Instead, it concentrates on general skills such as cataloging and information dissemination. In Zambia, there is a small job market for children's librarianship, considering that few public libraries in Zambia offer services specifically to children. Njobvu also notes that UNZA does not have faculty in their library science programs teach children's librarianship, and in particular the skills necessary to work with the vulnerable children served by the LLP.

During her time in Zambia as a Fulbright scholar, Mary Wagner worked with the UNZA Library and Information Services program. She describes this as a marvelous experience that challenged her to think in new ways and with new understanding about how she could best serve library and information science students. For one week during an introductory library science course for undergraduates, Wagner taught library services pertaining to children and children's literature. She described herself as totally unprepared to find that none of the students had ever seen a book intended for children. She observes, "And I found it was one of those experiences where you are telling people about something they have absolutely no experience with themselves, and they have no experiences on which to hang what they're hearing" (M. Wagner, personal communication, May 22, 2013).

SUCCESS: PROVIDING SERVICES AND PROGRAMMING TO VULNERABLE CHILDREN

Meyers believes that libraries can best serve youth by creating a safe and welcoming space that offers open access to various educational opportunities. LLP is dedicated to serving youth and children made vulnerable by circumstances, children who are excluded from many other social services, including out-of-school children, street children, and orphans. Recognizing the needs of these children, Meyers has taken the idea of providing a welcoming environment one step further: "We especially want to be 'home' for children who are homeless."

We feel that the best way to serve children, especially children who are dispersed, who don't have a strong center in their life or in their community, is by having a place just for them, that is especially for them—a place where they can come and connect with other people, that actually brings people together (J. K. Meyers, personal communication, January 8, 2012).

All of the interviewees spoke with high regard for this aspect of the LLP. During her stay, Wagner witnessed individual children and youth who have been touched by the Lubuto Library Partners and its many programs, such as Lubuto*Drama*, Lubuto*Arts*, Lubuto*Laptops*, and Lubuto*Mentoring*. "These programs give them access to creative and educational opportunities otherwise unavailable. I think for many individual kids, they have found a home, they have found support, they have had opportunities to explore and develop . . . in all those areas that Lubuto provides programming in—arts, drama, the computer technology piece, the books. I think for the individual kids that have been touched by the

FIGURE 11.3. Jane Meyers with individuals at the Fountain of Hope, the host partner of the first LLP library (Credit: Jane Kinney Meyers)

library and its programs, that's marvelous and wonderful" (J. K. Meyers, personal communication, January 8, 2012).

SUCCESS: PROMOTING LITERACY AND LIBRARIES

Lubuto Library Partners strives to support literacy through its Lubuto*Literacy* program, quality book collections, and preservation of Zambian children's and young adult literature. Lubuto*Literacy* provides interactive reading materials in Zambia's seven national languages using open-source software. The program operates in conjunction with the MESVTEE and enlists local teachers to work with youth to create lessons that follow the national curriculum. So far one hundred reading lessons have been created in each of the seven languages. Lubuto*Literacy* recognizes the importance of children reading in their first language and addresses the shortage of local-language reading materials. In 2012, LLP received a two-year grant from the All Children Reading program, a multidonor funding initiative supported by the United States Agency for International Development, World Vision, and the Australian Agency for International Development (AusAID).

LLP provides high-quality reading materials to support literacy development for the children and youth of Zambia. Njobvu mentions

FIGURE 11.4. Student and teachers working together to create lessons for *Lubuto*Literacy (Credit: Jane Kinney Meyers)

that a colleague from UNZA believes the LLP collections are of very high quality, particularly in comparison with other donated collections he has reviewed. LLP is working to preserve Zambian literature by creating a digital archive containing titles discovered in the collections of other institutions, such as the Library of Congress and Boston University's African Studies Library.

PROFESSIONAL DEVELOPMENT FOR CHILDREN'S LIBRARIANSHIP IN ZAMBIA

Since children's librarianship is currently not offered as part of the library and information science curriculums in Zambia, LLP serves in a consulting role to build the librarian profession. LLP has enlisted the help of library professionals and Voluntary Service Overseas volunteers to build capacity to meet national goals. Bwato explains that since children's librarianship is currently not part of the library science curriculum in Zambia, ZLS is looking at capacity-building opportunities outside the country, including UNISA in South Africa, a university that offers children's librarianship. With financial support, ZLS would be able to identify professional librarians who could go to South Africa for six to eight months to learn more about children's librarianship, particularly about working with children with special needs. Librarians could adopt and adapt these curricula to fit the needs of children's libraries in Zambia, including the Lubuto Library Partners.

LLP staff and volunteers have extensively presented and published on the topic of international library development. Staff has spoken at several library science programs, including San José State University and Drexel University, and at numerous professional conferences, including American Library Association, International Federation of Library Associations, Zambia Library Association, and Special Libraries Association conferences. The discussions at these presentations often focus on sustainability, the plight of Zambian street children, and the role libraries can play in achieving national development goals.

CONCLUSIONS

Zambian Partners Taking the Lead Role in Library Development

The success and sustainability of libraries depend on the community taking ownership, both literally and figuratively. Failure to work with the identified national library authority can lead to duplication of efforts and diminishment of the librarian profession within the partner country.

Lubuto Library Partners Working with the Zambian Government and Zambia Library Service to Mobilize Funds

It is important for library development initiatives to enlist help of library authorities and the government within the developing country to advocate for funds from both national revenues and international donors. This collaboration increases the chance of receiving financial resources, plus promotes sustainability.

Lubuto Library Partners Serving the Holistic Needs of Vulnerable Children

LLP recognizes that the basic needs of vulnerable children must be addressed before educational needs can be fulfilled. By offering a variety of programs that meet the educational, creative, and developmental needs of these children and youth, LLP proves that libraries can meet a wide variety of national development goals.

Creating a Cadre of Trained Children's Librarians in a Country with Limited Library Services for Children and Youth

Presently there is little professional training for children's librarianship in Zambia, based on the fact that there are few placement opportunities. With the creation of LLP, that situation can change, creating simultaneous opportunities for increased capacity building and career placement.

REFERENCES

Afwerki, I. (1997). Foreign aid works best when it's self-limiting. *Forum for Applied Research and Public Policy*, *12*(4), 68–71.

Bukenya, I. K. (2009). Public libraries. In I. Abdullahi (Ed.), *Global library and information science: A textbook for students and educators*, pp. 21–44. Munchen: K. G. Saur Verlag.

Easterly, W. (2006). *The white man's burden*. New York: Penguin Press.

Electronic Information for Libraries (EIFL). (2011). *Perception of public libraries in Africa*. Retrieved from: http://www.eifl.net/resources/perceptions-public-libraries-africa.

Hubbard, R. G., and Duggan, W. (2009). *The aid trap: Hard truths about ending poverty*. New York: Columbia University Press.

Kremer, M., & Miguel, E. (2008). The illusion of sustainability. In W. Easterly (Ed.), *Reinventing foreign aid*, pp. 202–253. Cambridge, MA: MIT Press.

Ochalla, D., & Bothma, T. (2007). Trends, challenges and opportunities of LIS education and training in Eastern and Southern Africa. *New Library World, 108*(1/2).

Organisation for Economic Co-Operation and Development (OECD). (2005). *Paris declaration on aid effectiveness*. Paris: OECD.

Ravichandran, N., & Rajashree, S. (2007). Financing sustainability and globalization: Theory and research. *Journal of Health Management*, 9(201), 201–222.

Europa Publications Limited. (2015). *The Europa world year book*. London, UK: Europa Publications.

United Nations. (2010). *Millennium Development Goals*. Retrieved from http://www.un.org/milleniumgoals.

World Bank. (2015). Zambia. Retrieved from http://data.worldbank.org/country/zambia.

TRAINING MODELS

PEACE CORPS TRAINING FOR SUSTAINABLE LIBRARY DEVELOPMENT PROJECTS

Marcy Carrel

In 1991, Laura Wendell arrived in the African village of Yikpa, Togo, to work on fisheries projects as a Peace Corps volunteer. She was equipped with a degree in biopsychology and had received Peace Corps training in language, intercultural skills, and fisheries. As time passed, she realized that what the villagers truly wanted was a library. Laura sought book donations, raised funds, and worked with dedicated community members until the idea became a reality. She later founded a nonprofit organization, World Library Partnership, and documented best practices in the publication *Libraries for All!* The library that Laura Wendell helped launch is a model of success in the history of Peace Corps volunteer library projects (Lawrence, 2000; Nixon, 2009).

Established in 1961 by President John F. Kennedy, the Peace Corps is a U.S. government agency that trains and sends volunteers to work and live in communities around the world. The mission of the Peace Corps is to promote world peace and friendship (Peace Corps, May 11). Since 1961, over 210,000 volunteers have served in 139 countries, and today, there are over 8,000 volunteers and trainees working in seventy-six countries (Peace Corps, 2012, *Peace Corps Performance*). Peace Corps volunteers are engaged in grassroots development through a variety of specific work assignments and activities. Currently, volunteers are assigned to one of six sectors or work categories: agriculture, community economic development, education, environment, health, and youth in development. Volunteer work projects vary widely. In addition to their primary work assignments, most volunteers are engaged in other work activities in their communities, such as English tutoring, youth sports, and library projects.

In fact, Peace Corps volunteers have been involved in library projects and library development throughout the history of the agency. In the early years, professional librarians were recruited and assigned to work in public and academic libraries in such places as Botswana, Colombia, Fiji, and Morocco (Office of Overseas Programming and Training Support [OPATS], 2013). Although librarians have not been recruited for over twenty years, volunteers have continued to engage in library projects of many types, more often as secondary activities.

Against this background, Marcy Carrel and Gail Wadsworth, the two librarians at Peace Corps headquarters in Washington, D.C., were presented with an opportunity to develop and improve training provided to volunteers engaged in library projects. "Focus In/Train Up," an agency-wide initiative, was introduced in 2011 to focus on key development sectors and train volunteers to excel in their work (Peace Corps, 2012). The OPATS led the initiative to redesign training. It has developed standardized training packages for specific project areas to guide field staff and facilitate training at Peace Corps posts worldwide. As of February 2013, about 180 training sessions and over 20 training packages had been developed and released to the field (OPATS, 2013). The *Sustainable Library Development Training Package*, written by the two Peace Corps librarians with input from the field and other experts, gives Peace Corps volunteers standardized training and guidance for library activities, as well as recommendations for appropriate resources to support library development in their communities.

Cross-cultural and intercultural skills are essential for successful Peace Corps service in any work sector. Regional recruiters and placement officers evaluate potential candidates on skills and suitability for service, gauging their ability to live and work in another country for twenty-seven months. Candidates who pass the final suitability review, as well as legal and medical clearances, receive invitations for a work assignment in a specific country (Peace Corps, 2012, *Live*).

After accepting an invitation to the Peace Corps, an individual travels to the country of service with a group of fellow trainees to begin a three-month training program. The intensive preservice training period includes technical, language, and cross-cultural training. Training is conducted by the local Peace Corps office, which includes both U.S. hires and local host-country staff. The Peace Corps headquarters in

FIGURE 12.1. The *Peace Corps Sustainable Library Development Training Package* is available for download at http://www.peacecorps.gov/library/pubindex/ (scroll alphabetically to the publication title)

Washington, D.C., through OPATS, provides programming and training guidance and resources.

While immersed in another culture, Peace Corps volunteers develop their intercultural skills in both informal and formal settings. During preservice training, most trainees live with host families to become more fully immersed in the local culture. When the training is completed, trainees are sworn in as volunteers and sent to their individual communities, where they work and live for the next two years. Volunteers are also given additional training opportunities at in-service training events throughout their service.

During preservice training, all trainees are introduced to the Peace Corps publication *Culture Matters*, and they are encouraged to use the exercises in the book throughout their service. During interactive training sessions, volunteer trainees distinguish between personal, cultural, and universal behaviors. They explore values such as formality, time, privacy, and communication along a cross-cultural values continuum and match behaviors to cultural values. They also identify possible adjustments to manage cross-cultural differences they may encounter during their service.

Successful Peace Corps service is predicated on successful integration into the community. Intercultural skills are essential to this integration process. As members of the communities where they work, volunteers are sometimes uniquely poised to understand the needs of the communities and facilitate a successful development project.

The co-authors of the *Sustainable Library Development Training Package* are both professional librarians and returned Peace Corps volunteers, with combined volunteer and relevant work experiences in Africa, Asia, Eastern Europe, and Central, North, and South America. These experiences provided an understanding of some of the realities faced by volunteers in the field and possible strategies for successful, sustainable library projects.

Developing training and resources to support volunteer library projects requires an understanding of both the volunteers and the types of library projects they become engaged in. The majority of volunteers are generalists, with little or no specialized work experience. The average age of volunteers in 2012 was twenty-eight, and 7 percent were over age fifty (Peace Corps, n.d., *Fast*). Over 90 percent of volunteers have at least a bachelor's degree.

There are no comprehensive statistics on the number, type, and description of volunteer library projects. Self-reported data in the 2012 Annual Volunteer Survey indicates that eight percent of volunteers are involved in library projects as part of their primary work assignment and 16 percent are involved in library projects as secondary activities (Peace Corps, 2012, *Annual*). Exemplary library activities are also sometimes highlighted in annual status report data that each country post submits to Peace Corps headquarters in Washington, D.C. The Peace Corps Partnership Program, a funding mechanism that some volunteers may utilize, provides a source of information for selected volunteer library projects (Peace Corps, 2013). Further, local U.S. media outlets may report on library projects undertaken by volunteers from their regions.

Such projects vary widely, but include book drives, creating infrastructure, developing classroom libraries and English-language collections, and putting together health clinic libraries. Volunteers working in all sectors may become involved in a library project, although it is more common among education volunteers. Recently, library work became a designated program activity for that sector. Here are a few examples of recent Peace Corps volunteer library projects around the world (OPATS, 2013).

Albania: A volunteer in a small city (population 32,000) worked with the local librarian to develop an English language children's collection in the public library, housed on the second floor of a cultural center. The volunteer also helped the librarian set up a children's weekly reading group and sent out an "Adopt our Library" call to friends and family to collect English language children's books for the library.

Namibia: An education volunteer teaching basic information science at a secondary school started a library renovation project with his thirteen basic information-science classes. This involved cleaning up and organizing an inherited school library of about 1,000 books that had fallen into disuse. Books were arranged by section, nonfiction books were cataloged using Dewey, and a circulation system was devised. Another volunteer helped install educational software in the computer lab of a public library.

Paraguay: Volunteers worked with municipal librarians to provide story hours to neighborhood children at public libraries to expand the role of the librarian and attract more children to the libraries.

Peru: An environment volunteer worked with his community to create about 6,500 ecological bricks (half-liter plastic bottles filled with inorganic trash), which are being used in construction of a multipurpose ecological building to serve as a library, eco-museum, and theater.

Swaziland: Health volunteers assisted "KaGogo" social-center managers with setting up a library and information center. They formed a library committee and assisted in training community members in cataloging, inventory techniques, and operations. KaGogo social centers were established in rural areas to address the growing number of children orphaned by HIV-AIDS.

While many Peace Corps volunteers engage in library projects around the world, most are not trained in library and information science. Volunteers are well versed in sustainable development, yet translating sustainability to the library context requires more specific consideration and training. The *Sustainable Library Development Training Package* was developed to address these needs. The purpose of the training package is to support and provide guidance to volunteers engaged in library projects and strengthen the work of volunteers in partnership with their communities.

The training package includes a series of detailed session plans developed by the Peace Corps librarians with input from field staff and training experts, ensuring that the training sessions meet the Peace Corps's interactive and learner-focused training style. The session plans follow the standardized Focus In/Train Up design, using a modified version of "4MAT" lesson planning with sections on motivation, information, practice, application, and assessment.* Training sessions are intended for a wide variety of circumstances and can be adapted, where noted, to fit specific cultural or local contexts. Sessions may also include handouts, trainer materials such as PowerPoint slides and flip-chart instructions, as well as supplementary publications.

Three library publications accompany the training package:

- *Libraries for All!: How to Start and Run a Basic Library*
  Laura Wendell. UNESCO. 1998. Reprinted with permission by Peace Corps. Updated version 2011. 79 pp.
- *Setting Up and Running a School Library*
  Nicola Baird. Heinemann/VSO. 1994. Reprinted by Peace Corps. 137 pp.
- *Sources of Donated Books for Schools and Libraries*
  Peace Corps. 2012. 26 pp.

These publications have been available for use by Peace Corps Volunteers for many years, but had not previously been part of any training, formal or informal.

Currently, there are eight sessions in the training package, in addition to an introductory document with background information and general guidance for Peace Corps staff trainers. It takes one-and-a-half to two days to deliver all the sessions, depending on the time devoted to optional field trips. Because posts have very tight training schedules,

*The 4MAT model is a learning framework that promotes student engagement. Access current materials at https://aboutlearning.com/4mat-training/4mat-on-the-go-training/

most participants would only be able to commit to a few hours during preservice training. The full package would probably be delivered at a dedicated in-service training later in the training cycle. Therefore, some sessions are stand-alone and most sessions are designed with few prerequisites. Trainers are also encouraged to give volunteers a copy of the training package itself, so that they can adapt the resources to provide training for community members. The key messages the authors sought to communicate through the training package are the importance of sustainability in a library context, and the availability of additional appropriate resources for a library project. Further sessions are prioritized accordingly and include the following:

PEACE CORPS RESOURCES FOR LIBRARY PROJECTS (PRESERVICE TRAINING)

This session prepares participants for library development projects by introducing them to Peace Corps Information Collection and Exchange publications that will be useful guides throughout the process.

Introduction to Sustainable Library Development
This session introduces the concepts of sustainability and "first, do no harm" in the context of library development.

Information Resources for Library Projects (optional)
This session is an overview of information resources available from the Peace Corps and outside organizations. These resources provide guidance for volunteers in developing and managing library projects.

Steps for Setting Up a Library
This session provides participants with a set of seven steps for setting up a library and provides practice for step 1, forming a library committee. A set of specific steps provides participants with a framework to consider, explore, plan, develop, initiate, and manage a potential sustainable library development project.

Organization and Classification
This session introduces the concept of organization through classification in the library context. Participants are given the opportunity to practice several classification systems that could be used in a local library. Organization and classification enable library resources to be easily located and used by library visitors.

Borrowing and Lending
This session introduces systems of borrowing and lending that participants could adapt to a local library project.

Supplementary Services
This session provides a brief overview of library supplementary services that may enhance and enrich the role of the library in a community.

Library Field Trip (optional)
This session gives participants an opportunity to visit at least one local library or resource center to observe and gain insights that would be valuable for library projects in their communities. The session is particularly helpful to introduce participants to local information resources and to encourage participants to establish contacts, begin networking, and gather ideas that might be appropriate for implementation in community libraries. The session is optional if it is not logistically possible to include a field trip during in-service training due, for example, to time or fiscal constraints.

SUSTAINABLE LIBRARY DEVELOPMENT FOR THE EDUCATION SECTOR

This session prepares participants for library development projects by introducing them to the Peace Corps Information Collection and Exchange publications that will be useful guides throughout the process. This session also introduces the concepts of sustainability and "first, do no harm" in the context of library development. As part of the Global Education Training Package, this session is intended as a requirement for all education-sector trainees or volunteers, and combines parts of three existing sessions. This session is the recommended single session for trainees or volunteers in any sector who are or will be involved in library projects, but do not have the opportunity to participate in the full training package.

The *Sustainable Library Development Training Package* was released in October 2012 and released again in February 2013 to include the new global education sector session. Field feedback is a critical part of the training rollout. All Focus In/Train Up training packages are written with input from the field and are released as "draft for pilot." After the training resources have been used at posts, feedback from training staff will inform further refinements of the training package, including development of additional materials to accompany the package.

The *Sustainable Library Development Training Package* was authorized for public release and is being promoted to the larger library community. All of the resources can be downloaded from the Peace Corps public website by scrolling alphabetically on this page of the "publications" section (http://www.peacecorps.gov/library/pubindex/). The hope is that the training can be adapted and used in many other library contexts. User feedback is encouraged.

The authors faced many challenges in developing the *Sustainable Library Development Training Package*. Succinct interactive training materials had to be written for U.S. adults with little or no background in libraries, and for those establishing libraries or facilitating library projects using one of many possible languages in any of over seventy-five developing countries. An initial challenge was lack of comprehensive information about current volunteer library projects. Thus, the authors began by compiling anecdotal information accumulated informally and seeking further sources of information to document the realities in which volunteers work.

The Focus In/Train Up structure and the time constraints of the Peace Corps training schedule presented further challenges. Although the session-plan format provides an effective standardized structure, it was at times difficult to follow exactly and to create "motivation," "practice," and "application" activities for each session. There was only time and space for information determined to be critical to any type of library project or situation. Sessions need to be adaptable to almost any context and include considerations of gender and potential differences in language and culture.

The training package includes and refers to several Peace Corps publications, including two older library-related titles, *Libraries for All!* and *Setting Up and Running a School Library*. Although the information in these publications is still valid and useful, their content does not seamlessly match the content of the training package. Some of the practices are unnecessary; some newer topics, particularly those involving technology, are not included. It is hoped that a new library publication will accompany the training package in the future.

A final challenge worth noting is that the training package has not been tested in the field. As with all Focus In/Train Up training packages, the *Sustainable Library Development Training Package* was released as "draft for pilot." The expectation is that posts will use resources to train volunteers, and some volunteers will adapt and use the resources to train community members. Feedback has not yet been received since the package was just recently delivered to Peace Corps posts.

One early success of the training package was the decision by OPATS to add a single two-hour session as required training for all Peace Corps volunteer trainees in the education sector. Library development is now a recognized activity for volunteers. The hope is that attention to library activities will continue to grow.

Another success was the authorization to release the *Sustainable Library Development Training Package* to the public and post the resources on the Peace Corps website. This is the first training package to be released publicly, and others are forthcoming. The authors hope resources can be used in the larger international library community and serve to encourage further discussion and collaborative efforts.

The development of the *Sustainable Library Development Training Package* and its use in the field offers potential personal and professional enrichment to different stakeholder groups: the authors of the training package, Peace Corps trainers, volunteers, and community members who participate in training. The authors are promoting the training package widely within the library community. They delivered a presentation in March 2013, shortly after the package was released publicly, to the Society for International Development, Washington, D.C. chapter, Development Information Work Group. A poster session and workshop presentation were conducted at the 2013 American Library Association Annual Conference in June. Additional presentations and articles may follow, furthering professional development opportunities for the authors.

The training package builds the capacity of Peace Corps trainers to provide library training. It also helps Peace Corps volunteers successfully engage in sustainable library projects and activities. Volunteers who then use the training package to facilitate training in their communities have the potential to improve and build their capacity as trainers for library projects. Finally, community members who are trained gain new skills, build capacity for sustainable library activities, and may continue by, in turn, training new community members to become involved in library activities.

The *Sustainable Library Development Training Package* has the potential to provide enrichment to the larger international library community. Sustainable libraries create advocates for libraries and enhance the professional status of librarians.

The authors of the *Sustainable Library Development Training Package* are fully aware of areas not adequately covered. They began planning for the next version before the digital ink was dry on the first. Innovation, library technology, budgeting, mobile libraries, and research services are just a few of the many topics that may be covered in a future version.

One possibility is to develop a continually growing collection of new sessions as a supplement to the core group, allowing trainers to choose those most relevant to their context. As mentioned, a manual to accompany the training package may also be developed, perhaps taking the form of a growing, dynamic set of resources available in digital format only.

In the near future, a new collaborative website, PCLive, will offer Peace Corps staff and volunteers worldwide the opportunity to share ideas and resources on training and development topics, including library projects. This forum will provide documentation of the work being accomplished and facilitate a community of practice around Peace Corps volunteer library projects. Collaboration will further enhance the quality and sustainability of library projects and activities.

REFERENCES

Lawrence, B. S. (2000). Obies and the Peace Corps: A longtime engagement. *Oberlin Alumni Magazine*, Summer 2000. Retrieved from http://www.oberlin.edu/alummag/oamcurrent/oam_summer_00/peace2.html.

Nixon, D. (2009). From North Carolina to KwaZulu Natal: World Library Partnership. *North Carolina Libraries*, *61*(4), 146. Retrieved from http://www.ncl.ecu.edu/index.php/NCL/article/viewFile/175/203.

Office of Overseas Programming and Training Support (OPATS), Peace Corps (2013). Internal files.

Peace Corps (n.d.). *4MAT Lesson Plan*. Retrieved from http://www.aboutlearning.com/.

Peace Corps (n.d.). *Fast Facts*. Retrieved May 11, 2013, from http://www.peacecorps.gov/about/fastfacts/.

Peace Corps (n.d.). *Mission*. Retrieved May 11, 2013, from http://www.peacecorps.gov/about/mission/.

Peace Corps (2012). *Annual Volunteer Survey Results*. Retrieved from http://files.peacecorps.gov/multimedia/pdf/opengov/2012_Annual_Volunteer_Survey.pdf.

Peace Corps (2012). *Live, Learn, and Work with a Community Overseas. Be a Volunteer*. Retrieved from http://files.peacecorps.gov/multimedia/pdf/about/pc_catalog_2012.pdf.

Peace Corps (2012). *Peace Corps Performance and Accountability Report Fiscal Year 2011*, (p. 19). Retrieved from http://files.peacecorps.gov/multimedia/pdf/policies/annrept2011.pdf.

Peace Corps (2013). *Find a Volunteer Project*. Retrieved from https://donate.peacecorps.gov/index.cfm?shell=donate.contribute.donatenow.

RECOMMENDED READING

Havard-Williams, P. (1994). Appropriate education for library and information science. *Libri: International Journal of Libraries and Information Services, 44*(1), 14–27.

IFLA International Federation of Library Associations. (2014). *IFLA, libraries, and development*. Retrieved from http://www.ifla.org/libraries-development.

IREX. (2014). *Beyond access—libraries powering development*. Retrieved from http://www.irex.org/project/beyond-access-libraries-powering-development.

McCreadie, N. (2013). *Library value in the developing world*. Retrieved from http://www.sagepub.co.uk/librarians/dw.

Mchombu, K. J. (2002). *Sharing knowledge for community development and transformation: A handbook*. Oxfam Canada. Retrieved from http://www.schoolnetafrica.org/fileadmin/resources/SharingKnowledge.pdf.

Meisler, S. (2011). *When the World Calls: The Inside Story of the Peace Corps and Its First Fifty Years*. Boston: Beacon Press.

Menou, M. J. (1993). *Measuring the impact of information on development*. Ottawa: International Development Research Centre.

Peace Corps. (1997). *Culture matters: The Peace Corps cross-cultural workbook*. Retrieved from http://files.peacecorps.gov/multimedia/pdf/library/T0087_culturematters.pdf.

Redmon, C. (1986). *Come as you are: The Peace Corps story*. San Diego: Harcourt Brace Jovanovich.

UNESCO. (2014). *UNESCO: Communication and information: Libraries* (http://www.unesco.org/new/en/communication-and-information/access-to-knowledge/libraries/).

CONCLUSIONS

International Librarianship: Developing Professional, Intercultural, and Educational Leadership compiles the experiences, adventures, and lessons learned from eighteen library professionals who engaged themselves with the world. Our colleagues demonstrated their commitment to develop intercultural expertise and sensitivities. They embraced their willingness to travel to distant countries to share their knowledge and learn from other global citizens, documenting their experiences in this collection of essays.

The twelve essays, grouped in five broad categories (Academic Exchanges, Fulbright Experiences, Information Literacy and Access, International Partnerships, and Training Models) span countries including China, Cyprus, Ethiopia, Guatemala, Hong Kong, Latvia, Morocco, South Africa, Tanzania, Tunisia, and Zambia.

The library profession encompasses values and guiding principles about learning, sharing, and supporting others to expand knowledge and understanding. The authors of the contributed chapters constructed their projects on the pillars of collaboration and exchange of ideas by designing new services and instructional modules, augmenting collections, lecturing, and organizing conferences.

Imagine travelling in northern Africa during the Arab Spring to explore religious diversity and bring back knowledge to your home campus to enhance dialogue about interfaith, interethnic, and interracial issues. Imagine travelling to South Africa with the goal of designing a sustainable strategic plan for the new Steve Biko Centre's library and archives, or partnering with librarians in war-torn Cyprus to promote shared understanding by facilitating a discussion between Greek Cypriots and Turks.

These experiences and the love of adventure that began as professional assignments demonstrate how the library profession prepared our colleagues and their global counterparts. For example, work in remote and rural villages provided access to textbooks that supported medical personnel in an Ethiopian hospital, awareness of the needs of vulnerable children in Zambia, and an understanding of global issues in the international library community through the work of librarians who developed training materials for the Peace Corps in the African village of Yikpa. Library faculty from City University of New York and their counterparts in Shanghai collaborated in an international exchange program that benefitted both universities and initiated opportunities and new visions for academic library services.

As demonstrated by these projects and the adventurous expeditions of participating librarians, international work requires survival skills and cultural awareness for connecting with local communities. This must be fundamentally based on natural curiosity and a sense of inquiry. International librarianship depends on diplomacy, deep respect, ongoing reflection, and acceptance of local customs and religions that at times may conflict with one's own personal beliefs.

The greatest rewards from such intellectual exchanges derive from acknowledging that nations are composed of people with dreams and aspirations. All authors aspired to develop communities of learning and trust by building confidence and promoting the benefits of shared values of education, medical care, research, and cultural awareness.

As stated by former Senator J. William Fulbright, founder of the Fulbright Program: "We must try to expand the boundaries of human wisdom, empathy and perception, and there is no way of doing that except through education. . . . The essence of intercultural education is the acquisition of empathy—the ability to see the world as others see it, and to allow for the possibility that others may see something we have failed to see or may see it more accurately," (United States Department of State, n.d.).

The contributors ultimately attest to earning personal and professional rewards from their international work. As a consequence, we have emerged more confident and knowledgeable about professional practice—as well as ourselves. We have come to realize that our community is our libraries—and our libraries, our world.

REFERENCE

United States Department of State. (n.d.) Retrieved from http://eca.state.gov/fulbright/about-fulbright/history/j-william-fulbright/j-william-fulbright-quotes.

CONTRIBUTORS

In 2009 **Marcy Carrel** joined Peace Corps–Washington as technical information specialist and serves as team leader for the Information Collection and Exchange unit in Overseas Programming and Training Support. She previously managed the Research-Information Center at Dayton Hudson Corporation for a decade before she joined the Peace Corps and served as a volunteer in El Salvador. Later she was an academic business librarian at the University of South Florida–St. Petersburg. Marcy has a BA from Carleton College, an MBA from the University of Minnesota, and an MLIS from the University of Wisconsin.

Sheau-yueh Janey Chao is professor and head of cataloging at the Newman Library of Baruch College, CUNY. She has published extensively, including books and articles in Asian studies, Chinese genealogy, library services to multilingual and multicultural populations, Chinese immigration and migration, and documentation and resource sharing in overseas Chinese studies.

Constantia Constantinou is dean of university libraries at Stony Brook University. She twice received Fulbright grants, once as a Fulbright Senior Specialist (2005), and then as Fulbright Scholar (2011). Constantia's work is known for crossing language barriers and overcoming political and ethnic conflict by building partnerships among internationally diverse communities. She has presented research and scholarly work on information literacy, library systems, and preservation and digitization in Canada, China, Croatia, Cyprus, Finland, Greece, Ireland, Korea, Russia, Spain, Turkey, and Ukraine. Constantia holds the faculty rank of Distinguished Librarian Professorship at the State University of New York.

Elizabeth Cramer is coordinator of bibliographic services at Belk Library and Information Commons at Appalachian State University. In addition to her MLS, she has an MA in French language and literature and an EdD in educational leadership. Elizabeth is active in the American Library Association's International Relations Round Table, and has served on several university internationalization and diversity committees. Research interests include international library development and the ALA Sister Library Initiative.

Beth Evans is associate professor in the library of Brooklyn College, City University of New York. She holds an MLS from Queens College, an AM in English literature from Brown University, and a BA from Brooklyn College. Her job includes implementing and promoting electronic resources and services, overseeing virtual reference services, coordinating the internship program, and other duties in reference, instruction, and collection development. In 2007, she was named a *Library Journal* "Mover and Shaker" for her work with social networking.

Lesley S. J. Farmer coordinates the librarianship program at California State University–Long Beach. She earned her MLS from the University of North Carolina–Chapel Hill and PhD from Temple University. Dr. Farmer has worked in school, public, special, and academic libraries. She serves as Special Libraries Association's Education Division chair, and won ALA's Phi Beta Mu Award for library education. A frequent presenter and writer, her research interests include digital citizenship, information literacy, assessment, collaboration, and educational technology.

Loida Garcia-Febo is president of Information New Wave, a nonprofit charitable organization enhancing education and access to information in developing countries. She is an expert in work with international organizations and services for multicultural populations.

Sandra Kendall is director of the Health Sciences Library at Mount Sinai Hospital in Toronto, Ontario. Since completing her master's degree in library science from University of Toronto, she has worked in corporate, public, and nonprofit libraries. Sandra has published in major Canadian journals and presented at library conferences, including those of the Internet Librarian and the Medical Libraries Association. Since 2008, she has been Library Science Program team leader with the Toronto–Addis Ababa Academic Collaboration.

John Lubans, Jr., independent scholar and visiting professor at the University of Latvia, has had a distinguished administrative career in academic research libraries. His most recent book, *Leading from the Middle and Other Contrarian Essays on Library Leadership* (ABC-Clio), was published in 2010. In 2011 he was a Fulbright Scholar in the Department of Information and Library Studies, Faculty of Social Sciences, University of Latvia.

Adriana McCleer is a doctoral student at the University of Wisconsin–Milwaukee's School of Information Studies. Her focus is intellectual freedom and information access. She has a master's in library and information science from the University of Arizona.

Michael J. Miller is professor and chief librarian at Bronx Community College, CUNY. He received a 2011 Fulbright-Hays grant supporting travel to the Maghreb region of North Africa to explore religious diversity in Morocco and Tunisia. His publications focus on educational technology and diversity issues within librarianship.

Chantal Phillips is student placement officer at Cape Breton University in Nova Scotia, Canada. She previously served as associate librarian at University of Guelph's Ridgetown campus. Chantal specializes in serving marginalized groups in remote, rural, and ethnic communities. Her work combines a background in development studies with an interest in Latin America and Africa. Chantal's current research projects include building civil society capacity for poverty reduction in Tanzania, open access and copyright issues related to knowledge translation and transfer for Ontario Ministry of Agriculture–University of Guelph Partnership, and "Veg Out! Crowdsourcing Keywords for Vegetable Crop Reports Online."

Ryan Phillips is assistant professor at the Newman Library at Baruch College, CUNY, serving as an instructional and business reference librarian. Ryan's research and publishing efforts focus on business information and entrepreneurship. He received his MLS from University at Buffalo, SUNY, and an MBA from University of Minnesota–Duluth.

Mark Aaron Polger is instruction and reference librarian at the College of Staten Island, CUNY, and information literacy instructor at ASA College in Brooklyn. He has worked in various capacities, as a medical librarian in a hospital, a children's librarian, and a cataloger at the Canadian Broadcasting Corporation in Toronto. His research interests include library marketing, library jargon, and the professional identity of librarians. He has published and presented internationally on topics such as library marketing strategies, student perceptions of librarians as teachers, and library signage.

Beth Posner is associate professor and head of library resource sharing at CUNY Graduate Center. In addition to writing about her experiences as a librarian in China, Beth publishes and presents on interlibrary loan best practices, the future of interlibrary loan services, and global interlibrary loan. She is also an active member of resource-sharing organizations including the internationally recognized IDS Project in New York State and the international group, Rethinking Resource Sharing Initiative. Beth received her MS in library service from Columbia University.

Kenneth Schlesinger is chief librarian at Lehman College, CUNY, a position he has held since 2007. He is board president of Independent Media Arts Preservation, which seeks innovative solutions to preservation of artists' videotapes and digital works. He also served as president of the Theatre Library Association. Mr. Schlesinger has received two Fulbright Senior Specialist Grants to contribute to international library projects: international copyright and strategic planning in Vietnam in 2005, and designing a library and archival strategic plan for the Steve Biko Centre in South Africa in 2011.

Ellen Sexton is a reference librarian and associate professor at John Jay College of Criminal Justice. She graduated from library schools at both University College Dublin and Queens College, CUNY. She holds a master's degree in environmental and occupational health from Hunter College, CUNY, and a bachelor's degree in physiology from Trinity College Dublin.

Stephen E. Stratton is head of collections and technical services for Broome Library at California State University–Channel Islands. He has been a librarian for over twenty years and has worked in academic and public libraries. Author of *Encyclopedia of HIV and AIDS* (2012, Facts on File), he is currently planning a return trip to Guatemala.

INDEX